Restoring Ceramics

Restoring Ceramics

JUDITH LARNEY

Foreword by N. S. Brommelle,
Keeper of Conservation Department,
Victoria and Albert Museum

Watson-Guptill Publications
New York

First published in the United States in
1975 by Watson-Guptill Publications, a
division of Billboard Publications, Inc.,
One Astor Plaza, New York, New York
10036

First published 1975 in Great Britain

Manufactured in Great Britain.

Library of Congress Cataloging in
Publication Data

Larney, Judith.
Restoring Ceramics.

1. Pottery—Repairing. I. Title.
NK4233.L37   738.1   75-4804

ISBN 0-8230-4547-1

Designed by Chris Pocklington

Contents

Acknowledgements

I wish to acknowledge the encouragement of Mr N. S. Brommelle, Keeper of the Department of Conservation, Victoria and Albert Museum in writing this book; and I should also like to express my gratitude to Miss Carolyn Zoeftig who dealt so patiently with all the typing.

Objects are illustrated in the book by kind permission of the following:

Fig. 14 The Victoria and Albert Museum; Fig. 15 Mrs R. van de Linde; Fig. 16 Mr T. C. Blofeld; Fig. 19 Mr Kirson; Fig. 20 Mrs Hudson; Fig. 21 Mr Cohen; Fig. 22 Mr M. Hodson; Fig. 23 Mr T. Wood; Fig. 24 Mrs H. Nelson; Fig. 25 Mrs J. Lennox.

Foreword

The number of reliable books on the restoration of art objects has always been small, mainly because it is difficult to persuade a busy expert to sit down and write about the subject in sufficient detail for it to be possible to apply the instruction in the absence of a practical teacher, working side by side with the learner. Apprenticeship with a working restorer is unquestionably the best way to learn, but where this is not possible, a practical manual of instructions written by the restorer and couched in the language that he, or in the present case she, would use in instructing the apprentice, is the next best thing.

Judy Larney, whose work brings her in daily contact with an enormous variety of fine objects in a great museum, has a gift for imparting her knowledge of restoration techniques with a practical immediacy. At the highest level, the empathetic feeling for the art object common to all good restorers is essential. These attributes can only be cultivated by experience in the studio. They cannot be learned from books.

N. S. Brommelle

Introduction

The aim of this book is to offer a guide through the range of processes that the restorer has to handle – from the initial cleaning to the final retouching of the ceramic. Tools, equipment and materials are all discussed; the names and addresses of suppliers are listed wherever possible. At the present time, methods and new materials are continually being developed and it is therefore not feasible to include all the products that are available on the market.

The basic requirements of the ceramic restorer are few and the materials mentioned in the text, if used with skill, should be sufficient to deal with every operation and most of the problems that are likely to occur. For anyone wishing to learn ceramic restoration, whether as a hobby or a profession, a basic knowledge of methods and materials that are used is essential. The problems that occur are many, and very rarely does one have a ceramic repair where each process, from cleaning onwards, is achieved without at least one difficulty arising. A so-called 'simple bonding job' can turn out to be little short of a nightmare if the object has 'sprung' out of true, and this is one of the problems for which a possible remedy is offered.

The demands on the restorer are many. He must be able to remove stains from a ceramic as well as bond a plate together so that all the breaks are perfectly aligned and barely visible. He will be required, amongst other things, to replace fingers, hands and flowers, and to do this his modelling skills must be of the highest quality. In addition to this the modelling must be adaptable to the style of detailing on the object being restored. His ability to handle and see colour must be acute enough to retouch an object to the extent of being either invisible or not offensive to the eyes. Modern synthetic resins have greatly assisted towards the rising standards of ceramic

9

restoration, but the greater percentage of success depends almost entirely on the precision and artistic ability of the restorer.

The first chapter of the book deals with the tools and equipment that will be required by the restorer. Specialist tools such as spatulas, scalpels and files are described, as are larger items including a dental drill, spray gun and compressor. The following chapters then offer information on the materials that are used for the various processes of restoration including bonding, filling, modelling and casting. Many adhesives used for bonding are readily employed in combination with other materials for fillings and modelling, and the combinations under which they are used is outlined.

The practical side of ceramic restoration is set out in as detailed a manner as possible, covering strapping, dowelling, filling and modelling on different types of ceramics. Only general methods can be offered as every individual will have his own system of working and will choose the way most suitable to himself.

The successful retouch will depend initially on the standard achieved with the previous processes. Any inaccuracies will be magnified as soon as the first layer of paint is applied, and emphasis has to be laid on the fact that one must aim for perfection at all stages.

General information is also given on the restoration of objects in a material other than ceramic including glass, jade, ivory and marble, and a comparatively new method of backing panels of tiles is fully described.

It is hoped that the information set down in this book will not only guide the amateur step by step through the whole process of ceramic restoration, but that the professional restorer will also glean further knowledge on his subject.

CHAPTER ONE
Tools and Equipment

This chapter will deal with tools (specialised and general), equipment and basic materials that will be required eventually for setting up a studio or workshop for ceramic restoration. A materials and equipment list is supplied at the end of the book which gives as much information as possible on where to buy items mentioned.

Any studio whether in a museum or in the home must have good north daylight. Whilst most operations can be performed in artificial light, the retouching of an object should be carried out with a north light, particularly if the object will be displayed in similar conditions. Objects that are likely to be exhibited in artificial light, probably fluorescent, should be retouched keeping in mind the conditions under which they will be shown. Good ventilation is essential if spray equipment is going to be used. Ideally, for all retouching operations, whether by spray or brush, one should have a separate dust-free room, with extraction fans and a filtered intake of air. This would minimise the danger to the operator from the effects of solvent fumes. Dust particles will ruin an otherwise perfect retouch which may have taken a considerable time to achieve. One should also have adequate storage space, either cupboards or shelving, and as much surface working area as possible, preferably topped with plastic laminate.

Old cigar boxes or wide-necked jam jars are useful for storing small tools such as files and also brushes. Polythene bottles are essential for keeping solvents in, and they can either be bought new or one can use washing up liquid bottles thoroughly cleaned out. All bottles must be clearly labelled, and if one is working in the home where there may be children, they should be kept either locked up or well out of reach when not actually being used.

Handtools can be collected over a period of time to suit the individual needs or preferences of the restorer and for specific jobs as they may be required.

Fig. 1 illustrates a selection of the type of tools that are used. The following items listed will probably all be needed at some point in time. A palette knife, in stainless steel, with a blade of three to four inches for mixing up resins, etc. For modelling up and filling, metal spatulas obtainable from a sculptors' suppliers are the best tools to use. These come in a wide range of sizes, and the smallest and medium double-ended ones are the most useful to begin with; others can be collected over a period of time. Boxwood modelling tools, which are considerably cheaper, are obtainable from most artists' materials stores. A good selection of files will be invaluable as they will be required for a great deal of work. Ordinary Swiss needle files either round, triangular or flat, coarse or fine, can be found in most good ironmongers or watchmakers' and jewellers' supplies shops. Diemakers' and riffler files are a little more difficult to find, but if you can get them they are invaluable. They come also in various sizes and shapes, and two or three of these, particularly the curved ones, will be a good investment. You will also need a pair of fairly long tweezers, in stainless steel, for applying cotton wool swabs where contact with the hands should be avoided. Surgical scalpels are much safer to use than razor blades but must still be handled with a certain amount of care. The best combination is a No. 15 blade with a No. 3 handle and a No. 23 blade with a No. 4 handle. Blades and handles are available in most artists' shops, chemists or ironmongers. They also make a long-handled scalpel which can come in useful at times, but one should avoid straight-edged blades as they are impractical. Care should be taken when putting new blades into the handles as they are very sharp and can give a nasty cut. It is usually safer to insert the blade only half way and then push the tip of the blade against something solid to lock it firmly into position. Alternatively the whole operation can be carried out by gripping the blade in a pair of small pliers and inserting it this way. By doing this one will avoid the possibility of the fingers slipping if pressure is used to push the blade home. These scalpels should be held at a fairly flat angle across the area being pared or cut, as too much pressure on the tip, if used vertically, may cause the blade to snap and fly up in the air. Replacement blades are easy to obtain, but as they become blunt fairly quickly a Carborundum stone for sharpening them up is a good economy.

Small pliers, the long-nosed variety, will be essential for many jobs including pulling out old dowels and rivets. A pair of small wire cutters will be required, as will a junior hacksaw with spare blades.

Dental probes are extremely handy and can either be bought new from a dental suppliers or acquired second hand from your dentist. These, if blunt, can also be sharpened up on a stone. Items such as a small hand or pin vice, callipers and small G-clamps can be

collected as they are required. A bench vice will be essential for
many jobs, such as cutting through dowelling which has to be held
firmly. A medium-size vice will be quite sufficient, and one can buy
the type that clamps on to the bench, for permanent fixtures can
sometimes get in the way if space is limited.

Other small essential items are as follows. A Sellotape dispenser
with half and three-quarter inch tape. Plenty of cotton wool, paper
towels or tissues and rag. Scissors, squares of glass or tiles for mixing
up on. Polythene sheeting, A good selection of wet and dry abrasive
papers from Grade 100 up to 1000, and a pack of Flex-i-grit which
is a plastic-backed fine abrasive. A tube of Solvol Autosol, a mild
chrome polish for surfacing fillings and cleaning. French chalk. *Figure 1*

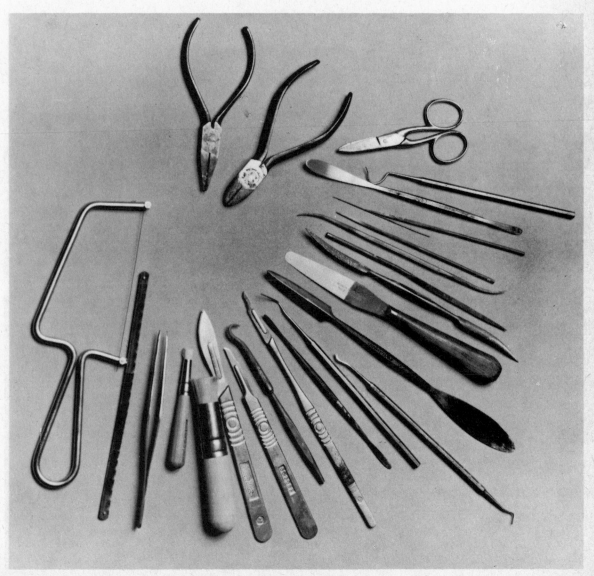

Wooden sticks (orange or cocktail sticks will suffice). A collection of paste and jam jars, yoghurt cartons, and various sizes of polythene containers. The latter are used for soaking objects in and can be acquired as they are needed. A sandbox will definitely be needed, and this can be any suitably sized container filled with sand. Working materials include: kaolin powder, titanium dioxide, Polyfilla – both ordinary and fine surface, plaster of Paris, and Plasticine.

The shelf life of polyester and epoxy resins will be extended if they can be kept in a refrigerator, but it is not advisable to have them in close proximity to food.

Larger items of equipment include a dental drill, a set of scales, and spraying equipment. The dental drill can be either hand or foot controlled with a flexible drive and chuck sizes down to zero. This is an invaluable piece of equipment for grinding down fillings, surfaces and drilling dowel holes. The drill itself will cost around twenty-five pounds depending on the quality, but on top of this you will need to buy drill points and burrs, and for porcelain and glass you will need diamond-tipped points; the average price of the latter is about one pound fifty pence per point. Any dental suppliers will have a wide range of these from which to choose, and the types most widely used are a medium-sized disc for cutting, a tube drill, a small ball tip, a thin point and one with a larger surface area for grinding (see Fig. 2). Ordinary carbide abrasives will be suitable for grinding down resins.

If used correctly, these diamond-tipped points will last for a considerable time. The point should always be kept cool whilst drilling, if not it will become so hot that the diamond tip will be burnt off; and it is therefore essential to use cold water either as a

Figure 2

continual drip on to the area and drill tap, or by having the object actually immersed in the water. When operating with the object itself under the water, care must be taken not to have more than just the drill tip under the surface; otherwise with a hand controlled motor, it is possible to receive an electric shock if the handpiece gets wet. It is not necessary to apply great pressure when drilling with diamond points, they cut extremely well into porcelain and will virtually do the job themselves with a minimum of force.

A spray gun and compressor will eventually become an essential item of equipment, as spraying a large background area can be quicker than be retouching with a brush. There are many firms that produce portable compressors at reasonable prices, and one has to shop around to choose the one that will fit all requirements. These include being a reasonable weight for moving around and being relatively quiet, particularly if being used in the home. It will also need to reach up to forty pounds pressure, and have a gauge that will clearly indicate this; if possible a filter should be fitted to deal with the moisture build up, and it should have a foot-controlled switch. Spray guns are a matter of personal choice and there are various makes to choose from on the market. All are adjustable to spray from a wide area down to fine line and you should select the one that feels most comfortable in the hand and is easy to clean out efficiently. As with all equipment, it must be kept in good condition which means that immediately after use it is thoroughly cleaned through every time with the relevant solvent to prevent the nozzle blocking with dry paint. Nothing is worse than being all prepared to spray, only to find that this is blocked – causing one to spend up to an hour cleaning it out. When using the spray gun, particularly at home, one must be certain of adequate ventilation, as solvent fumes can be distressing and dangerous in an enclosed area.

Some grades of Araldite, such as AY103/HY951, need to be measured accurately by weight, and here you will need a set of scales. They need to be very accurate as the proportions of this resin are crucial. It is possible to pick up scales in second-hand shops, and new sets of gramme weights can be purchased for around five pounds from laboratory suppliers. As an alternative to scales, one can measure out the proportions of resin to hardener by volume using measuring cylinders or spoons.

CHAPTER TWO
Cleaning Agents and Solvents

De-ionised water is preferable for all washing, soaking and cleaning purposes, and a museum workshop will probably have a unit available. The suppliers, mentioned in the materials list at the back of the book, also produce a small portable unit which would probably suit the individual restorer. A substitute for de-ionised water is distilled water which is available readily from garages and chemists, and this would be preferable to tap water.

For removing old overpaint and some adhesives such as shellac and Araldite, Nitromors is most effective. This is a paint stripper, basically a methylene chloride, and can be used on old adhesives and repairs where other solvents fail. It will remove paint from terra cottas, plaster casts and marble. Absorbent bodied ceramic should always be pre-soaked in water which will prevent stains from old adhesives, such as shellac, from being drawn into the body and causing discoloration under the glaze. Marble can be safely degreased with Nitromors before full cleaning treatment. The water-washable variety of Nitromors should be used normally, but a spirit Nitromors is also available and may work where the former does not.

Lissapol NBD is a non-ionic detergent and its uses are as a wetting agent and for general cleaning for ceramics as well as ivory or bone. It is used in a low concentration of up to one per cent with water as the solvent. It is also miscible with white spirit.

A white spirit and soap solution will clean a great many surfaces, particularly greasy ones. It can be made up easily with a fifty-fifty mixture (one pint total) of white spirit and water plus one teaspoon of Lissapol or Fairy Liquid. Whenever used, this solution must be well shaken as it separates out when left standing. Solvol Autosol is a mildly abrasive chrome polish. Applied with a stiff-bristled toothbrush or stencil brush, it will dispose of ingrained dust often found on badly abraded glazes and also surface dust from parian wares and marble. It will also polish up silver rims often found on ceramics and can be used for final surfacing to an Araldite filling and for retouches. Residual powder is removed with white spirit.

Jenolite, which is basically a phosphoric acid, may be used for the removal of surface metal stains of the type found on ceramics where rivets have been and for rust marks. It can be purchased in liquid or paste form from hardware stores. It must not be used on surfaces such as marble which it will etch.

Ammonia will generally remove copper or brass stains from places where rivets have been, and is applied on a swab of cotton wool. Sepiolite (100 mesh) is a magnesium silicate similar to Fuller's Earth. The Sepiolite pack method was originally designed for cleaning marble, but can be successfully adapted for removal of stains from ceramics. It is mixed with de-ionised water to the consistency of a wet paste. The object should firstly be degreased either with acetone or Nitromors, then pre-soaked in de-ionised water, and some of the mixture smeared with the hand or a soft brush over the entire surface to ensure that the paste will make contact everywhere. The paste is then applied evenly over the object with a palette knife to a maximum depth of about a quarter of an inch. As the water evaporates out of the mixture, the dirt or stain will be drawn from the object into the Sepiolite. This will take about twenty-four hours, depending on the atmosphere of the room, when the Sepiolite pack will begin to dry out and crack up, separating itself from the object. The dried out Sepiolite is then picked and brushed off and the surface washed with de-ionised water. This treatment may have to be repeated two or three times until the stains are completely removed. For oily or greasy stains, white spirit or Shellsol 'A' can be substituted for the water, again carrying out the treatment as many times as is necessary to draw out the stains.

If this solvent fails then one will have to use a stronger method. Hydrogen peroxide can be used on harder bodied ceramics. A solution of one part hydrogen peroxide (100 vol) to three parts of water plus one or two drops of ammonia is a suitable strength. Here again the object concerned must be pre-soaked in water. By doing this the water will act as a barrier to prevent the stains from being absorbed into the body of the ceramic. Peroxide swabs applied to stains on a dry object can move the stain either through to the other side or to another area. When the object has been pre-soaked in the water it is placed in a shallow polythene container, and cotton wool swabs are soaked in the peroxide solution and patted on to the discoloured areas using a pair of tweezers or forceps. They are left for two or three hours and the process is repeated for as long as is necessary. If the treatment takes more than a day, the object should again be placed in water overnight and the process started again next day. When the stains are completely removed the object is thoroughly washed in water and allowed to dry out. The strength of the solution can be increased if it is thought necessary, but a close watch must be kept on the object, particularly if there is any gilding on the glaze, as this may be affected by the peroxide if left for any length of time. Peroxide is also used for removing dirt and stains from the break edges of porcelain, etc., for if these edges are not clean they could mar an otherwise perfect bonding operation. Again the soaked cotton wool swabs are applied all along the break edges, and replaced after two or three hours until all stains are removed (see Fig. 3).

Ordinary domestic bleaches and detergents should be avoided when cleaning ceramics. They can have adverse effects such as discolouring a glaze, fading lustres and causing a glaze to crackle.

A selection of solvents will be required for various cleaning and thinning uses. One meets a variety of old adhesives which will have to be removed before a new restoration can be carried out. Animal glues are quite common, and soaking in warm to hot water will eventually break these down. No object should ever be plunged directly into boiling water, or indeed boiled up in a receptacle on a hot plate or gas ring. The object should first of all be placed in water that is about blood heat, to allow it to absorb the warmth, and then hotter water can be added to this. The temperature should be kept by draining off part of the water as it cools and adding more hot water until the adhesive finally gives way. If the adhesive is not

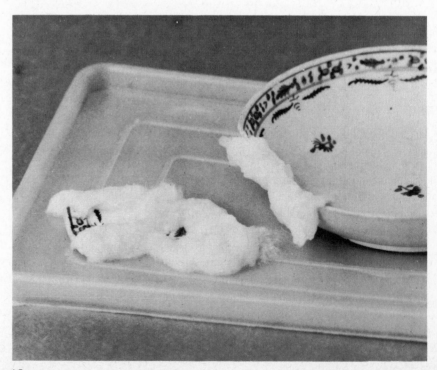

Figure 3

18

water soluble, it could be a cellulose adhesive such as Durofix, which will break down with acetone, either by soaking the whole object in the solvent, or applying cotton wool swabs. Shellac can become almost insoluble with age and is often very difficult to remove. It can be broken down with either a fifty-fifty solution of ammonia and industrial methylated spirit, or with Nitromors. When using Nitromors on an absorbent body such as earthernware, if one is going to immerse the object, it should be pre-soaked in water. Nitromors, on contact with shellac, often creates a nasty purple stain which could become absorbed into the body and leave marks under the glaze. It is not often necessary to immerse an object completely in the stripper, for if it is applied along the joint it will eventually eat down into the old adhesive and the joint will part. This action is usually speedy, and if the object or pieces can be placed in either an enclosed polythene container or a bag, this will prevent the Nitromors from evaporating and thus increase the length of time it can work on the old adhesive.

Rubber solutions such as Evo-stik can also be removed with Nitromors, turpentine or toluene. White spirit or turps substitute will be needed as thinners for polyurethane and can also be used as a cleaning agent. A cellulose thinner such as Gipgloss will be required as a solvent for the polyurethane PU11. It is also a solvent for most stoving enamels. Other chemicals or solvents that may be needed at some point are acetic acid, hydrochloric acid, ethyl acetate and Cellosolve (2-ethoxy-ethanol). It is advisable to keep all these chemicals and solvents in a cool and if possible fire-proof cupboard, and great care must be taken when using chemicals as they can cause damage to skin and clothes.

CHAPTER THREE
Adhesives

There are so many adhesives on the market these days that it is quite difficult to keep track of them all as they appear and to test them. The adhesives that are discussed in this section are those most commonly used in museums and by private individuals, generally for their reliability. There is to my knowledge no adhesive that will not discolour in time, and this is one of the main problems that the ceramic restorer has to live with. Some, of course, do not discolour so quickly, especially if used in a very thin layer, or to such a degree as others, and in order to separate the good from the bad tests are carried out in the museum laboratories. For the ordinary person, these tests are not possible to make easily, but if one is trying out a new adhesive, it would be wise to bond two pieces of ceramic or even ordinary plate glass together, leave it two or three months in strong light, and then observe the degree of discolouration, if any. This will also help to test the strength of the adhesive before deciding whether to use it on more important objects.

The availability of some resins is also becoming more difficult, and it is not always easy to buy small quantities of materials, which can be very inconvenient where some, such as epoxy resins and hardeners, have a limited shelf life. If these resins can be kept in a cool place such as a refrigerator, this will help the problem. It should be remembered that if a refrigerator is used, it should be for the resins only, as it is not wise to mix these with food. Care should also be taken when using epoxy resins such as Araldite, as one can develop allergies and dermatitis from it. Hands should always be washed thoroughly after using the resin. Most firms supply technical sheets with their adhesives and other products which will give a guide to the procedure for use and the precautions that should be observed.

ARALDITE

The most suitable grade of Araldite is AY103 and hardener HY951. It must be very accurately mixed, the proportions being 100 parts of resin to 9 parts of hardener, and this is where one will require a set os scales. The hardener HY951 is hygroscopic and must therefore be mixed in a dry warm atmosphere. When mixed it should be allowed to stand for ten to fifteen minutes for the chemical reaction to get under way. The most convenient amount to mix at a time is 50 of resin to $4\frac{1}{2}$ parts of hardener, and a yoghurt carton, thoroughly clean, is an ideal receptacle to use. This mix, if kept in a well-sealed container with either silica gel or rice to absorb any moisture, and then placed in the freezer compartment of the refrigerator, can be used over a period of four to five days. It obviously becomes tackier towards the fourth day, but in this state can be extremely useful for bonding ceramics with fairly porous bodies where in a more liquid state it could cause staining under the glaze. By keeping and mixing the Araldite in this way, only the amount required for a specific job need be taken out at a time, thus reducing wastage. Titanium dioxide white pigment is generally mixed with the resin for binding, as this does help retard any yellowing tendencies and will tone more readily with the ceramic.

The same resin AY103 can also be used with the hardener HY956, which is basically the same as the 951. This hardener is stated to be less likely to cause allergies or dermatitis and also its mixing proportions are easier to manage, being 20 parts hardener to 100 parts resin or approximately 1 to 5. This means that it can be measured quite accurately without scales, and one can use measuring spoons, either plastic or metal, which one can buy easily from stores selling kitchen equipment. Storage and use is the same as for the AY103/951, and its bonding strength appears to be comparable, also it is liquid enough for pouring into moulds for casting.

These two grades of Araldite are not obtainable in ordinary shops, and apart from a museum supplier can only be ordered or purchased directly from the manufacturers. The third grade of this resin, which can be bought from most hardware or do-it-yourself shops is the two-tube variety, obtainable in small or large sizes, and one can also buy it in two-kilo containers, but only from the manufacturers. This grade, although convenient being a fifty-fifty ratio of hardener to resin, is very much thicker and of a yellow brown colour from the beginning, tending to discolour further after a comparatively short time. Mixing in white pigment does retard this a little as with the other grades, but one needs quite a quantity of the pigment to get a white base colour. It is too thick to pour into small moulds under normal conditions, but warming it will liquify it sufficiently to fill uncomplicated moulds.

QUICK-SETTING EPOXY ADHESIVES

Here again there are many different products on the market and it is difficult to know which are the most reliable. Although they can have a great many uses they are possibly not as dependable as the epoxy resins mentioned previously. Most set in around five to ten minutes and are fully cured in twenty-four hours. They enable a joint to be held together whilst setting which can be invaluable where a speedy first-aid repair is required. Time can also be saved by using them to set dowels in place before bonding on legs and arms, etc. As with epoxy resins, these adhesives can also cause skin irritations, and instructions for their use should be followed carefully, particularly for the removal of surplus adhesive from the hands.

POLYVINYL ACETATE EMULSION (PVA)

Here again, various products and grades are available. Mowlith DMC2 plasticised is made by Hoechst Products, but is possibly not available in small quantities; there is also Vinamul 6525 which is more or less the same quality but available from museum suppliers. Evo-stik Resin 'W' is also a polyvinyl acetate emulsion, and although produced as a wood adhesive is basically the same material, its advantage over the other two being that it is readily available from most hardware shops in convenient quantities. For ceramic restoration its main use is for bonding earthenware and terra cottas. If the break area is slightly damped before the adhesive is applied, it will ensure a strong bond and small chips of glaze can be bonded down speedily and without danger of staining. It can also be used for bonding small, badly broken glass objects, as it does not discolour, and sets quickly under relatively light pressure. This would only apply to glass objects that will spend the rest of their lives in a show case, for not having as much strength as Araldite would have on glass, it would not stand continual handling or use. Soapstone and ivory can also be bonded with it. It is extensively used in museum galleries for bonding down ceramics that are displayed openly. It is readily soluble in acetone or water.

CYANOCRYLATE RESINS

These adhesives, of which Eastmans 910 and Cyanolit are examples, polymerise under pressure in a few seconds. This means that with an object broken in many pieces, the amount of adhesive between the joints would be minimal, thus avoiding a build-up which some other adhesives might produce. For a perfect bond, these adhesives require an absolutely clean, smooth surface and are thus ideal for use on jades, coral and some glass.

SINTOLIT (transparent)

A polyester resin which sets in approximately ten minutes, enabling an object to be held in position while setting, helping one to achieve perfect alignment. Although this adhesive is used mainly for marble and stone restoration, it can be invaluable for bonding earthenware ceramics such as plates, dishes and tiles. It discolours quite badly and must therefore be kept well within the perimeter of a break

22

edge, but because of its great strength, very little adhesive is required to achieve a good bond. Its viscosity prevents it from being drawn into the porous body of earthenware and thus avoids the possibility of staining by creeping under the glaze. White pigment can be added, and also a little kaolin, and this will make a very strong quick-setting filling for emergency uses, though only for shallow missing areas. It is very easy to mix, the ratio of hardener and resin being, according to the container, 'one teaspoon of resin to one coffee bean of hardener', and so one has some leeway so far as accuracy is concerned.

CHAPTER FOUR
Materials for Fillings

There are few ready-made compositions on the market and in general they are not entirely satisfactory owing to shrinkage, too rapid setting, poor surface quality or one or other of the problems that beset the ceramic restorer. Some restorers use china clay which could be feasible for individual components, but there is of course a great disadvantage here of having to deal with shrinkage, and where a component has to be added to the object, there is still the problem of the invisible joint. This will probably involve dowelling, filling and retouching so there does not seem to be any advantage in going to these great lengths. Ideally one requires a composition that is easy to handle and can be modelled to a fine degree, and therefore be relatively slow-setting under normal conditions. Also it must have a good unpitted surface, not too hard or brittle to file down, which can then be rubbed to a superfine finish. Added to this it should not be affected by changes in atmosphere, or if being used on domestic ware, by immersion in hot or cold water, or by heating. Obviously the ideal is rarely available and so one must compromise, and the following compositions will in fact cover most needs; the one which comes closest is the Araldite resin which can be used with several aggregates.

Araldite AY103 and hardener HY951/956 is the resin used for most fillings on porcelains, bone china, stoneware and all hard bodied ceramics. The two-tube variety can also be used in the same way. Titanuim dioxide alone can be used with the resin which will produce a very white filling, but a combination of the white pigment to give colour and barytes or kaolin is generally favoured. Sufficient titanium white is ground into the resin to produce a white base, and into this the kaolin (or other filler) is mixed to the required consistency which will be more as a putty, being firm rather than sticky and paste-like. One should be able to work it between the fingers, and with a dusting of dry kaolin powder, can roll it out on a piece of glass just like pastry to any degree of thickness required. If modelling up a free-standing part like an arm, a supporting wire or dowel will be needed for the initial application. This should be allowed to set, and further modelling can be applied on top. The composition sets slowly enough to allow ample time for fine modelling, and this is best achieved when the 'putty' is at a rubbery stage which it will reach after about one and a half hours. In this state, it is often less clinging and easier to handle, and any excess can be removed with a sharp blade. Obviously, when using Araldite with titanium dioxide and kaolin to model up with, one must be patient and build up in degrees. Too much applied at any one time may sag under its own weight and distort the modelling. Tools used for detailing can be dipped in methylated spirit which will stop them dragging, but care must be taken not to make the surface too liquid. Where the area to be filled is on a plate rim or somewhere similar, strips of Sellotape or Plasticine, lightly dusted with French chalk, will be suitable to use as supports.

For earthenwares Polyfilla, which is a vinyl-reinforced cellulose filler, makes an ideal filling material. The most successful proportions for mixing Polyfilla are as follows: 100g of Polyfilla to 40ml of water mixed thoroughly to a stiff putty consistency. If a ground colour is desired, dry pigment can be added, but as the mixture will dry considerably lighter than it will look when wet, a sufficient quantity of pigment must be added to reach the required tone. One's judgement here will improve with practice. If a rough or coarse texture is called for, a small quantity of fine washed sand can be introduced. Polyfilla when rubbed down can often have a pitted surface due to air bubbles and, after the first levelling down of the surface, a second layer will probably be required. If a very fine, super smooth ground is needed, there is now a new product on the market called Fine Surface Polyfilla, described as a vinyl-based spackle and supplied ready mixed. This can be applied on top of the ordinary Polyfilla and will produce a very fine surface for retouching which will probably not need priming. The ordinary Polyfilla is also used for modelling up missing parts such as hands and feet, etc., which will remain as permanent restorations on earthenwares or terra cottas, but can be cast in an epoxy resin if the object is porcelain.

Polyvinyl acetate solid, Rhodopas 'B', is a clear resin which can be used for small fillings on jade, coral and glass. This is a far more complicated method for fillings and is more suitable for the museum workshop where equipment and the material are more likely to be available. One will need a hot plate made from a 500W element inside an inverted 'Pyrosil' casserole dish, connected with an emergency regulator (see Fig. 4). A quantity of the resin is melted on the hot plate and if a coloured filling is required, dry pigment is added and thoroughly ground in until the desired tone is obtained. The melted resin is scooped up with a stainless steel palette knife, spread out on to silicone paper and allowed to cool. It is worthwhile, when involved on this part of the process, to mix up a selection of different colours which can be used at some future time. The area to be filled is first painted with polyvinyl acetate emulsion to provide adhesion. A chip of the prepared PV acetate solid is then placed in position and pressed down with a heated spatula (the same as used by picture restorers), using either silicone or Melinex film as a barrier between the spatula and the resin. Silicone paper will leave a matt surface, which with Melinex film, will be glossy. When cooled, the paper is peeled off and the process repeated until a satisfactory filling is achieved. The resin will only adhere to the pre-coated area, and any excess can be pared off with a scalpel blade.

This material can be very useful for building up missing chips in either glass, jade or coral as the colour can be matched perfectly and will not yellow. It is not an easy method to use; it has the added inconvenience of requiring special equipment which the private individual will probably not have and, as the procedure may only be carried out rarely, will most likely not wish to invest in. However, it is possible for the museum restorer, who will probably have the

Figure 4 equipment to hand.

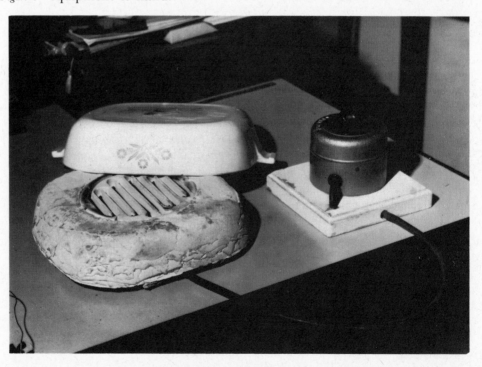

CHAPTER FIVE
Resins and Materials for Casting and Moulding

CASTING

Of the Araldites mentioned in the previous section, the grade AY103 with either hardeners HY951 or 956 is suitable for casting. A little titanium dioxide white pigment is thoroughly ground into the resin to give a good white base for retouching. Araldite in a large quantity will generate quite a lot of heat, so if the mould to be filled is of a large size, i.e. requiring 50g or more of resin, then care must be taken to keep the mould cool, or bubbling will occur and spoil the cast. This can be avoided by either filling the mould in more than one stage, or by placing the filled mould in a container or polythene bag in the refrigerator and leaving for two days until the curing is well on the way and no more heat will be generated. The above grade of Araldite is very liquid when first made up, and will pour easily into even the smallest mould.

Plaster of Paris, of good fast-setting dental quality, is also used from time to time, but generally for larger casts such as the whole base of a vase. It can be greatly strengthened by impregnation with Araldite resin. For this operation, the plaster must be absolutely dry and gently warmed. One coating of Araldite resin is then painted on evenly and this will be drawn into the plaster. The process is repeated, warming the plaster before each painting, until the resin is no longer being absorbed into the plaster; the cast is then left for the resin to cure. This will provide a good, hard, non-absorbent surface upon which to retouch, as well as strengthening the plaster.

Polyester resins, either for casting or embedding, can also be employed, and there are several types on the market, most of which are available from artist and sculpture supply shops. These resins are very clear and water white, and most of them appear to retain this

27

quality for a considerable time before yellowing; they could therefore have their uses for some glass restorations. The only problem with them is that they are sometimes a little unpredictable, and one can be left with a sticky surface which on the odd occasion either does not harden at all, or will take some time to do so. However, they cast well in both rubber latex and silicone rubber moulds.

The only casting resin that is virtually guaranteed not to discolour at all, is an American epoxy called Maraset. The problems here are first, its availability, and second, that it must be heat cured at 71° centigrade for sixteen hours. The latter problem means that missing areas cannot be cast directly on to the object, but must be cast separately and then fitted on. In some cases this is entirely feasible, but on other occasions the work that would be involved is often not warranted. It is a pity, because this resin is so clear and colourless that it would otherwise be perfect for filling in and making up missing areas on glass objects. Colour mixes in very well with the resin and various aggregates can be added to simulate different surfaces. Mixed with ground white glass it resembles marble very closely and is used quite a lot in sculpture restoration.

White Sintolit (Sintolit bianco) can be used for very quick casts of a small but uncomplicated nature. Although the resin is liquid enough to pour, one has to fill the mould very speedily as it does set very quickly.

MOULDS

The two materials mentioned earlier, rubber latex emulsion and silicone rubber, are I think the most satisfactory, as between them they will cover all the possibilities. The most commonly used for ceramic restoration is rubber latex emulsion. It is extremely flexible and therefore ideal for moulds of hands, flowers and anything of an intricate nature. It should not be used on metals (unless well lacquered), ivories, marble or painted surfaces as it has a high ammonia content and will affect these. Also, for the same reason, it should be allowed plenty of time to cure, twenty-four hours or longer depending on the thickness of the mould; otherwise the ammonia if still present will upset the curing of the casting resin.

For a very small mould the latex is painted on layer by layer, allowing each coat to coagulate before the next is applied, until the required thickness is reached. The surface should be dusted with French chalk before peeling off to prevent the rubber curling back and sticking to itself. For larger moulds, or where more rigidity is needed (e.g. an area of plate rim), cotton flock, fine sawdust or wood-flour can be added to the latex. The quantity added is sufficient to obtain a paste consistency, so that the mixture will not sag whilst setting. The area from which the mould is being taken should first be pre-coated with one layer of neat latex to ensure that air bubbles will not be present and the whole area will be covered. The flock and latex paste is then applied evenly, the thickness of the

28

layer depending on the size of the mould and the rigidity required. For large moulds where distortion may occur, a plaster of Paris 'mother' can be made to ensure the mould holds its shape when filled with the casting material. This must be made while the rubber mould is still on the object, which can be brushed over with clay slip to make the parting of the plaster from the latex easier. The inside of a latex mould should be dusted with French chalk before being filled.

Silicone rubber can be used on surfaces where it is not possible to use the latex. It is nowhere near as flexible as the latex and would not be suitable for making a mould of a hand as it will not peel back on itself. It is more suitable for moulds of a relief nature with very little undercut. Surface moulds of flowers and leaves can be made successfully, and it does have the advantage of setting in around half an hour. Most resins will cast well in silicone rubber, but it is advisable before using epoxies or polyesters to heat cure the mould for about one hour at 100° centigrade.

Paribar, a dental moulding material, can be used for press moulds, as can Plasticine. The Paribar needs to be warmed or softened in hot water and is kneaded to uniform plasticity in this state and pressed on to the area to acquire the correct impression and then withdrawn. It hardens on cooling and can be reused if softened again in hot water. It does not require a parting agent.

CHAPTER SIX
Bonding

Before the bonding process begins, the restorer has to decide on the adhesive that is to be used, which will depend on the object to be put together and the method to be followed. First of all, though, he must be quite sure that he has taken all the steps leading up to this process. All the break edges must be perfectly clean and free from dust, grease and loose particles. The minutest fragment of glaze, old adhesive or indeed any foreign body will prevent a perfect bond. Any staining should also have been removed, for no matter how perfectly an object has been bonded together, if the break edges are stained, then the repair will be more than obvious with no way to disguise it, save by overpainting or spraying which would not be satisfactory. Methods and the relevant solvents required for removing old adhesives have been mentioned, as have processes for removing stains, and these steps should have been followed. Obviously one will come up against a few objects where it is impossible, for unknown reasons, to draw out stains even though every feasible method has been tried, and here one has to make do with what one has. In this case if it is a private job, the owner or, if belonging to a museum, the curator, must be informed of the problem and the decision of whether to accept the stain or to overpaint the break has to be made. If an object has been soaked in either water or solvent at some point during cleaning, it must be given ample time to dry out before bonding.

A trial run of assembling pieces together without adhesive is a very good practice to follow. One can then check where the missing areas are, and it also offers a good indication of the way pieces fit together. The order of the final assembly can be decided, starting with the pieces that locate well with one another and building up until all the pieces are fitted in. One of the biggest dangers with a multiple break is the locking out of any one or more pieces and this can be avoided by making a pre-run, using Sellotape to hold the pieces in position. Numbers can be put on each individual section if deemed necessary, so that if the sequence is followed, no mistakes should be made.

Locking out does tend to happen more often on bowls and vases than on plates, this being due to the fact that it is probably more difficult to detect. Fig. 5 illustrates some examples of bonding, and Fig. 6 shows the locking out of a piece. Very often one can get to the stage of having only two pieces left, either of which can be fitted individually, but not both together. In a case like this, there is a definite advantage to bonding an object in one session rather than in separate units in which the adhesive is allowed to cure before the whole is assembled. In the former case, it may be possible to release the strapping a fraction on the adjoining breaks to allow the last pieces to be eased in, and then readjust the tape to pull all the breaks together. If this cannot be achieved without force, then the only alternative is to take the object apart and start again, which could be very time consuming and, if the adhesive had been allowed to set on some sections, not that easy either. The break edges themselves could also be damaged in the process of removing the adhesive.

When the decision has been made on the course of bonding to be followed, and the adhesive has been selected, the next step is to check that all components are entirely clean, including the restorer's fingers. Break edges should be given a final wipe over with acetone to remove any grease or dirt which may have got there during the piecing together with the tape in the trial run.

BONDING WITH ARALDITE

With Araldite AY103, and hardener HY951 or HY956, it will not be necessary to warm either the adhesive or the ceramic, but a little warmth may help the two-tube variety of Araldite to flow more thinly. When the pieces are being joined with adhesive they need to be under a certain amount of pressure which has to be maintained and this is where strapping is necessary. The tighter the joint is, the less visible it will be. It is often helpful to have strips of tape ready to hand and one strip already sticking by one end to the pieces being joined. A Sellotape dispenser is an invaluable item of equipment to have as it enables the tape to be cut off to the required lengths easily with one hand. It can be very inconvenient if it becomes necessary to put the ceramic down in order to tear off a piece of tape.

Where the broken edges fit cleanly it will only be necessary to apply the adhesive to one edge. Too much adhesive will prevent the two surfaces from locking together and providing a close fit, and could cause a cumulative error where there are many pieces to join. When joined firmly together the adhesive on the one edge will be

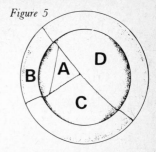

Figure 5

A to B and then C, as this piece will fit in with A and B with no problem

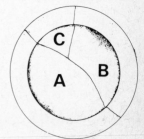

A is bonded to B. Then C to A and B. Piece D is then bonded to A, B and C

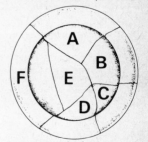

A, B and C would be bonded together as one unit. E bonded to F and then D to E and F. The two separate sections then bonded together

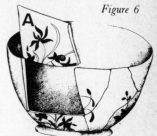

Figure 6

The piece marked A is locked out. This is where making a trial run can be invaluable.

31

pressed out thinly between the two surfaces forming a good union, and any surplus will be expelled along the edge of the crack. This can easily be removed when set with a sharp knife. Should any adhesive have spread on to gilding, it should be wiped off at this stage with a solvent such as acetone or methylated spirits, for if allowed to set hard the gilt will be pulled off while trying to remove the Araldite. If the ceramic is of a coarse nature then the adhesive should be applied to both edges ensuring that it will enter any cavities, thus providing a good consistent union. The adhesive will also be squeezed out at the end of the breaks, possibly on to a broken surface that is not immediately going to be bonded, and this may occur where the object is being assembled in separate units. It is essential to remove any such beads of adhesive before they set so that they do not form any obstruction when another piece is fitted to this surface.

Before starting the bonding process, the chosen Araldite should be mixed ready with titanium dioxide and if required a little colour, and the Sellotape dispenser or ready cut strips of tape should be close at hand. A small strip of tape is taken and one half stuck into the china at a right angle to the break, with the other half folded back over the thumb. The adhesive is applied to the break edge and the two pieces are pressed together until they are seated perfectly together. The folded back piece of tape is then pressed down with the thumb across the joint and affixed to the opposite piece. At this stage, tensioning of the tape is not necessary as this step is just to anchor the two pieces together so that they can be handled without the danger of parting company. Another strip of tape is applied in a corresponding position to the back, and then more tape can be added, this time using tension. Sellotape will stretch when pulled and then slightly contract, so that if it is firmly affixed to one side of a break and then pulled tightly up and over the joint and pressed down on the opposite side it will draw the two halves firmly together. It is essential to make absolutely sure that the joint is perfectly aligned, and this can be checked by running the tip of the finger nail across the break to detect any discrepancy, which can then be adjusted with a little pressure by the fingers in the right place or even by wriggling the two parts together so that more adhesive is squeezed out and the joint becomes closer. With a multi-assembly, this procedure is followed through whilst systematically applying the tape to the front and the back, taking care to keep the tensioning even and always pulling the tape at right angles across the breaks. It is of utmost importance that accuracy is maintained throughout; checking each joint for perfection; a minute error can build up when joining several pieces and it could be possible, by being a fraction out at the start, to be unable to get the final pieces to fit accurately into position. Sellotape is also useful to pull together an opened crack. In this case it may be necessary to warm the object either in a low temperature oven or just locally on the area of the crack with a hair-dryer. The Araldite AY103/HY951 or 956, with a small quantity of titanium dioxide ground in, will on contact with the warm ceramic become very fluid and run in into the crack; this then is pulled together with the Sellotape using the same strapping method, making sure that the two sides are perfectly level.

In some cases, for example a broken cup handle, pieces to be bonded may be too small to strap with Sellotape and then it may either be a question of balancing the two pieces one on top of the other in a sandbox or a wedge of Plasticine. A pad of Plasticine may also be used as a bed for one piece of china whilst the other piece is wedged and held in position with another pad, ensuring that the Plasticine does not come into contact with the break (see Fig. 7).

A whole handle or the knob of a lid can be held in position with tape. In this case the tape is stretched over the handle and pulled down to the sides of the cup, making sure that the tensioning is equal for both sides, otherwise the handle might move out of true while the adhesive is setting. The cup itself can be either set in a sandbox or wedged between two lumps of Plasticine to prevent it rolling. Balancing an object in such a position to enable a part such as a limb, which may be too small to dowel or strap, to be bonded on is made easier with a box or bowl of sand. The object is placed on the sand so that the broken surface is horizontal. Obviously a lot of experimentation will have to be done to find the exact angle at which to place the object, so that the broken limb will balance perfectly and not fall into the sand. Once the correct point of balance has been found, the break edges are wiped over with acetone and then adhesive is applied on one edge and the two pieces are carefully pressed together, taking care not to alter the position of the main part of the object in the sand (see Fig. 8). A dowel will help to hold the two pieces together and prevent movement, and will at the same time provide an even stronger joint. Plasticine has a great many uses for supporting limbs and extending pieces whilst they are setting, but one has to use one's ingenuity to achieve success where some problems may look very difficult to solve.

The introduction of fast-setting epoxy resins has alleviated this problem to a certain extent, as they can be used where it is impossible to balance a part, but where it would be possible to hold the joints together for five minutes until the adhesive has set. Perhaps they should not be used where any great strength is required as they may not be as reliable as Araldites. However, these adhesives do mean that the use of complicated counterweights can in most cases be dispensed with.

Araldite AY103 will take up to twenty-four hours to harden sufficiently for the tape to be removed from the object, and wherever possible it should be left for two or three days to give it maximum curing time.

A note should be made here about removing Sellotape. This

Figure 7

Two pieces of a cuphandle. Right hand piece with dowel in place. Left hand piece (dowel holes hidden) set in Plasticine

Both pieces set tightly together, both supported by wedges of Plasticine

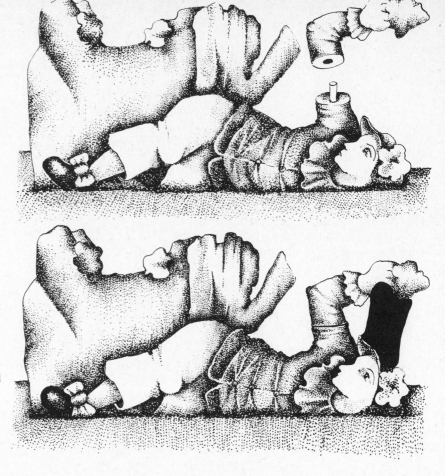

Figure 8

Figurine balanced in sand
to correct angle. Dowel
holes drilled in both break
edges and dowel in
position in lower half

Top half of arm in correct
alignment with lower half.
Wedge of Plasticine is used
for extra support to
prevent any possibility of
movement

should be done carefully and not torn off without thought or loosely
attached glaze or enamel may be brought with it. Particular care
must be taken on gilded surfaces which in some instances are easily
lifted. In the case of gilded surfaces or indeed where there may be
any doubt as to the stability of a glaze, swabbing with white spirit
will remove the tape without there being any need to pull it off.

If the ceramic body is of an absorbent nature, there is a risk in
using Araldites as an adhesive, particularly the AY103 grade which
is of low viscosity, and it could get drawn too far into the body and
cause staining under the glaze. The two-tube variety would be more
suitable to use here, or alternatively the AY103 can be mixed with
white pigment and then left for a while until it becomes viscous, but
still fluid enough to enable a tight joint to be achieved.

SINTOLIT (transparent)
For earthenwares, Sintolit is a useful adhesive and it has the added
advantage of setting relatively quickly so that an object can be

34

assembled in a short space of time. This adhesive, a polyester resin, is of a fairly thick consistency and is already a yellow colour to begin with, but will turn much browner in setting, and for these reasons must be used with discretion; but one can still achieve a very tight joint which will be immensely strong. For heavy earthenware plates, bowls or tiles, it is ideal as one can hold the pieces in position whilst the adhesive hardens off.

The two break edges to be bonded must be fitted together without the adhesive as a trial run, since there is not time for any major readjustments after about four minutes when the Sintolit begins to gel. Only a small quantity of adhesive will be required as it will squeeze out thinly along the break surface under pressure. The proportions of the resin to hardener are, according to the container, one teaspoonful of resin to one coffee bean of hardener which does give one quite a lot of leeway in mixing, and by adding slightly more hardener one can get the adhesive to set a little quicker; alternatively less hardener will slow setting. Ten minutes does not sound a long time, but if you are holding two pieces of ceramic together under pressure, it can seem like hours, so it is important to place yourself in as comfortable a position as possible. The adhesive is mixed and applied to one surface keeping well within the perimeter of the break, and the two halves are brought together. Slight wriggling of the pieces under pressure will help to squeeze the Sintolit along the crack and enable the joint to be tighter. When the two pieces are correctly located, truly aligned and as tight as possible, they must be held without movement until the adhesive has set. One or two previously attached strips of Sellotape can be used in the same manner as for Araldite bonding, for in the first three or four minutes there will be time to pull them across the joint. If this can be done, it will reduce the amount of pressure one has to apply with the fingers, and if the break edge is in a horizontal position, only the lower half will need to be held, leaving one hand free to test the remaining Sintolit to see when it finally sets hard. Any excess adhesive can be removed with a sharp blade when it has set hard. Sintolit is an extremely good adhesive for earthenware tiles, whether Delft, Portuguese, Islamic or whatever. Quite often the ceramic body is very porous, and unless used in a very tacky state, which would probably prevent a good tight joint, Araldite would almost certainly get drawn into the earthenware to a certain extent and cause staining under the glaze.

It must be remembered that if a stoving enamel is going to be used for retouching, then Sintolit should not be used as an adhesive on the same object, as it will soften and possibly part company at around 100°C.

For smaller earthenwares and terra cottas, polyvinyl acetate emulsion is a strong, quite fast-setting adhesive that is fairly easy to use, and it will not soak in or leave a stain. There are many products on the market, one or two which have been introduced in the section on adhesives, but perhaps the most convenient type to purchase is Evo-stik Resin 'W'. This is sold primarily as a wood adhesive, but is quite suitable for earthenwares. It is obtainable in polythene containers from a few ounces to a gallon in most do-it-yourself or hardware shops. For smaller earthenware objects it is of great use as it will set in a few minutes under pressure, and an object can thus be built up in one session. To obtain a maximum bond, both break edges should be slightly damped with water, the adhesive is applied to one edge and the two pieces are brought together immediately and pressed tightly against each other and held for three to five minutes. After this length of time the unions between the two pieces should be sufficiently strong to enable them to be put down, preferably supported in a sandbox for about half an hour to allow the polyvinyl acetate to set fully. Using this adhesive does not really allow any time for major adjustments so one must be absolutely sure of a perfect alignment at the first attempt. By damping the break edges this will allow an absolute minimum of movement with the two sections before the adhesive coagulates. Should a mistake be made, acetone will remove the adhesive without any difficulty. Small fragments such as chips or glaze can easily be bonded on quickly with this adhesive and loose glaze can also be held down with it. Soapstone which does not like many adhesives can be bonded very successfully with PV acetate, used in the same manner as above, but here it would not be necessary to damp the edges. The same applies to ivories for which it is also excellent.

In museum galleries it is used extensively for sticking down ceramics and other objects which are displayed free standing on furniture. The furniture will have a plate glass top on to which the object is stuck to avoid damage to the surface or veneer, but it is quite safe to bond an object straight on to a marble top. The adhesive is usually applied first round the perimeter of the base and this should give enough surface area for a strong bond. If the object has a hollow, shallow base it can be first filled with Polyfilla to provide a flat surface, or if a deep hollow, a wooden block can be fitted. Either of these methods will provide sufficient surface area to make good contact. A wooden insert would be bonded into the hollow base with PV acetate and allowed to dry thoroughly before being stuck down on to the furniture top.

Polyvinyl acetate is chosen for this job because it is easy to remove with either acetone or water, which is important as objects are changed around fairly regularly, and also should someone choose to try and make off with a vase, it is preferable that the object if it comes off, comes off intact, and does not leave its base stuck to the furniture, as it could do if Araldite or Sintolit were used.

Whichever adhesive you choose to employ, bonding is not the easiest process in restoring ceramics, but you will obviously improve with experience. For the person just beginning it is advisable to practice as much as possible on worthless items, if necessary buying tea or dinner plates and breaking them. This will also give one a good idea of how to use the Sellotape, as tensioning tape is not as easy as it looks and also requires practice. Every step in the restoring process is vitally important, with each depending on the other, and starting with cleaning the object. If the joints are still dirty, it will not matter how well the pieces have been bonded, they will still show. Equally, if the break edges are out of alignment and are stepped, not only will they be obvious, they will in turn make the fillings difficult to apply and impossible to disguise. One must never be content with a second-rate attempt and, providing the circumstances allow it, one should aim for as perfect a job as one's ability will permit.

Cyanocrylate resins such as Eastmans 910 and Cyanolit can also have their uses but are somewhat limited. They are very convenient if one has many smallish fragments in a material such as jade or coral, where the break edge would be clean and smooth. It needs such a surface for a successful bond. A tiny drop of the adhesive is put on one edge and the two pieces are held under pressure between the fingers for about ten seconds. Here again one has to be quite sure of a perfect alignment at one attempt as in ten seconds there is no room for adjustment or indeed any movement either; if one does move either piece within this time the contact will be broken and no bond will be achieved. If this happens and the two pieces in fact do not stick, then acetone will clean the surfaces for another attempt. One does have to use quite a considerable amount of pressure, and although only for ten seconds it is surprisingly difficult to maintain it evenly, while holding small pieces between the fingers; it is quite easy to underestimate one's strength and go a little too far in the wrong direction causing the two edges to slide. This can of course cause damage by chipping the edges, so one must be very careful, particularly if bonding glass.

CHAPTER SEVEN
Dowelling

If one feels that reinforcement to a joint is necessary, this being where the object is either large and heavy and where a great deal of strain will be put on the joint, then the best method to use is dowelling. This means inserting a stainless steel or brass pin into both sides of a break. A porcelain plate or dish with larger than normal dimensions and broken straight across the centre in two halves will require such strengthening for its own safety, in view of the strain put on the single joint. Any object of this size will probably be thick enough to allow room for drilling dowel holes, and on a dish of twelve to eighteen inches in diameter two holes should be sufficient. The best positioning for the holes would be at the thickest area on the base, as shown in Fig. 9. If blobs of wet paint (acrylic colour is ideal) are applied to one half only where the holes are required, and then the two pieces are positioned together, the points will be indicated on the opposite half. This marking method will obviously work for any joint that is being dowelled together. Once the marks are made, the dowel holes can be drilled with diamond points, beginning with a small point and graduating to a larger one. The size of the hole depends on the dimensions of the object, and if similar to the dish mentioned previously one would be using a dowelling rod of about $\frac{1}{8}$in. in diameter, and the drilled hole would have to be slightly larger than this to allow room for an adhesive. The depth of the hole need be no more than $\frac{1}{8}$in. as this will give sufficient anchorage. The stainless steel or brass rod is cut to the correct length and to check that it is right a trial fitting should be made. The break edges of the ceramic should also have been cleaned. For smaller objects the bonding process would be one of those mentioned previously, either strapping or balancing, and one would probably require both plus the assistance of a suitably large sandbox.

The lower half of the dish is placed vertically in the sand with the dowelled break edge horizontal, bedded in so that it does not move (see Fig. 9). Araldite mixed with enough kaolin to give it substance is inserted into the two holes and the steel rods are placed in position, wriggling them round so that the adhesive makes contact with all surfaces within the hole and excluding air trapped at the base of the hole. The same process is carried out with the opposite half taking the same precautions with the dowel holes, and on this half Araldite with just a little pigment is applied to the break edge. Sellotape strips can be placed in readiness on the lower half, back and front, to be pulled up over the joint. The second half is then lowered into position and correctly aligned using enough pressure to achieve a relatively tight joint. The Sellotape already applied is pulled up over the joint and stuck down on the opposite half; this will help prevent any movement. More strapping can now be added to pull the joint even tighter, checking with the fingernail to make sure that there is no stepping, also being sure to keep the tensioning consistent both at the back and the front of the dish. When satisfied that the joint is perfect, the dish is left for the adhesive to set hard making sure that it is safely balanced in the sandbox. The tape is removed and any excess adhesive is cut away with a sharp blade. If the object is earthenware, then the same procedure is followed for the dowelling, but Sintolit can be used as the adhesive, and in this instance less strapping would be required.

For broken off limbs such as arms, hands and heads, or wherever there is sufficient surface area, a dowel of stainless steel or brass can ensure a very strong joint. The same procedure can be used for marking the dowel holes as used with the dish, and the dimensions of both the hole and the rod will be relative to the size of the broken off limb and the surface of the break area. The angle of the holes on both halves must correspond and should be kept central within the perimeter of the break surface.

When drilling porcelain or hard bodied ceramics one must remember to drill under water or with water dripping on to the area, for if not kept cool, the diamond points will be burnt off.

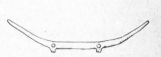

Figure 9

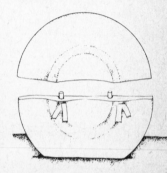

Dowel holes drilled into the break edge at the thickest area

Lower half of plate bedded in sand. Dowels are in position and two strips of tape ready to be pulled over joint

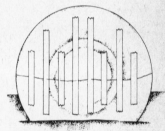

Plate bonded together. Balanced in sandbox and with Sellotape drawn across the break to ensure the joint is tight

CHAPTER EIGHT
Filling and Modelling

Invariably when your object has been bonded, there will be chips or apertures that need filling in. Taking in the first instance hard bodied ceramics, such as porcelain, the material most used for this job will be Araldite. Either the AY103 and HY951 or the two-tube variety are used in the same manner. Into the required amount of Araldite white pigment, titanium dioxide, is mixed to provide a good white base colour. It is possible also to mix in other pigments at this stage if a coloured filling to match the ceramic is required. This colour should be mixed rather on the light side as it will become very much darker when the filler powder is mixed into the resin. It should also be remembered that this resin will discolour in time and however well matched the filling is to the ceramic, it will start to yellow after a few months, and should always be retouched. However, it does often help to have an already toned background for retouching.

Having decided on either a toned or white filling, and having mixed the pigment into the resin, the filling powder is added. This can be either barytes (barium sulphate), kaolin powder or plaster of Paris. Barytes is a very heavy substance and will give a more plastic result, but kaolin, though lighter, will provide an equally good filling and is also much easier to obtain from the local chemist. Both are used in exactly the same way and there is no difference in the quality of the end result. A small quantity of Araldite and pigment is set on one side and into the remainder, the kaolin or barytes is mixed, until a putty-like consistency is reached. For modelling-up, or filling larger gaps, it should be pliable enough to handle in the fingers; one should also be able to roll it out like pastry where thin strips for leaves or flower petals are needed. For surface chips that

40

are very shallow the mixture should not be quite so stiff, but more stickiness on good adhesives is essential and this quality tends to be lost with the more putty-like composition. As most objects will have both shallow surface chips and deeper ones, including rivet holes, the filler can be mixed up in two separate grades, filling the shallow areas first and then adding more kaolin for the stiffer putty.

Small shallow chips, such as those that run along the edge of a crack or bonded joint, will retain this Araldite filling perfectly well so long as it is really pushed in thoroughly. It should be applied with a small metal spatula pressing the filling well down into the cavity and keeping the surrounding surface as clean as possible. If one takes care and time to get the fillings in neatly, a lot of hard work will be prevented later, remembering that grossly overfilled small chips will need considerable filing or cutting down which could result in them being lifted out of their seating under too much friction. It is most unlikely that one will achieve a perfect filling at the first stage, and work when the resin has set is unavoidable; on balance, therefore, it is probably better fractionally to overfill and then to cut down, rather than to underfill and have to add a second layer which will involve another day for curing plus surfacing. Wide but flat chips are often more difficult to fill, particularly where the surface is very smooth. Given enough area, one can rough these up with a fine diamond point, or bore one or two mooring holes which will give a key for the filling. Generally, though, if a small amount of neat Araldite (that is without the kaolin powder) is smeared over the surface this will give sufficient purchase to the putty which is applied on top with a spatula.

Rivet holes appear very regularly for filling and here the stiff putty should be packed in thoroughly, bit by bit, ensuring that air at the bottom of the rivet holes does not get trapped under the filling. If wished, some smoothing down can be done after a couple of hours, when the filling will have partially set, using a silk rag dipped in methylated spirit. With very shallow fillings, if an attempt to smooth them with the meths is made before the Araldite has partially or fully set, this will often result in too much being removed. Missing gaps in rims of plates or bowls can be either made up with the help of a mould or with a simple support. For flat missing areas of up to an inch width on a ceramic in such places as a plate rim, the neck of a vase or the perimeter of a bowl, Sellotape strips will make a good foundation against which to press the filling. A double layer of tape will give less under pressure than a single layer, and the tape is easily separated from the set Araldite leaving a smooth surface. It also has the advantage of being transparent so that one can see if all corners and edges have been adequately filled. An alternative to the tape would be to use a backing of Plasticine. The Plasticine should be rolled out flat to a size large enough to cover the aperture and to overlap the surrounding ceramic on which it is pressed. If dusted with French chalk, it will separate quite cleanly from the Araldite filling. One can also use Plasticine to make a quick pressed mould where Sellotape would not be suitable. This might occur where the surface is curved, fluted or with a slightly raised pattern. On a curved surface of more than an inch, Sellotape will tend to form a straight line and not assume the shape of the curve. The Plasticine is rolled out to a thickness suitable to the size of the job, and large enough to cover the aperture with a margin. If the surface is fluted or has a raised pattern the mould will be pressed on this side, but if the area is flat then it is generally more convenient to take the mould from the underside. The surface is damped where the mould is being taken, to prevent sticking, and this will be on an area corresponding to the missing gap; the Plasticine is then evenly pressed down, allowing an overlap at the top edge which is gently bent over so that the rim will be clearly impressed in the Plasticine. The whole is then gently eased off, and if the Plasticine was thick enough it should hold its shape. The mould is then fitted over the aperture and the overlap margin pressed into the ceramic to which it will hold. It is lightly dusted with French chalk or can be coated with a separating agent, and the Araldite putty is pressed in with a spatula. In all cases, before the putty is applied Araldite with only white pigment mixed in is smeared on to the break edges receiving the putty, thus ensuring a secure bond between the filler and the ceramic. The surface of the filling should be as level as possible and can be smoothed with a little methylated spirit on the finger or with a spatula.

There will be the occasion when a mould or proper support is not possible to use. This might happen with the broken spout of a teapot, and unless an identical one is available one will have to rely on direct modelling. The main missing part can be built up in steps, allowing each application of putty to cure, using strips of Plasticine to support each layer. Once there is a foundation of Araldite putty, the spout can be built up to an approximate shape. When the composition has set hard, the surface can be brought to a final finish by first filing if necessary and then using coarse to fine grades of abrasive paper.

The finish of a filling is very crucial; one cannot afford the slightest discrepancy however minute, as this will show up under the retouch. This is perhaps the most tedious exercise as one can spend many hours carefully rubbing down the surface. Depending on how much excess composition there is, filing is the first step, using first a fairly coarse then finer grade file. Grooves will be left by a file so one must be careful not to take the filing down too far with grooves below the level of the surrounding ceramic. Once the bulk of the surplus is removed, abrasive paper is used to get the surface smooth. Grade 320 wet or dry silicone carbide paper is of a suitable coarseness to begin the operation. The paper is used in smallish folded pieces, so that one can use an edge or corner, and the motion of rubbing is from the filling out towards the edges of the

42

surrounding glaze, rather then across the glaze to the filling. This way one will avoid any damage to the ceramic, for if this happens it is irreparable. The utmost care must be observed to avoid this occurring, and if the rubbing down is carried out with patience and sense, this should not happen. Using the paper folded with a small strip of square and gripped between the finger and thumb, one has far more control over where the abrasion takes place, and this is important where the filling meets the edge of the ceramic. One cannot afford to abrade beyond this point.

Blemishes such as pin holes or small cavities may appear in the filling at this stage and there may be need for one or more further applications of Araldite putty to remedy this. The surface of the filling must be perfectly uniform with the surrounding ceramic and one must keep on refilling and rubbing down until this perfection is achieved. As mentioned before, the slightest inaccuracy will be more than apparent when the retouch is applied. The ultimate surface can be obtained by using the finest possible abrasive paper such as grade 1000 or 1200 wet or dry, or Flex-i-grit which is a plastic-backed abrasive and extremely fine. After this the surface is polished with Solvol Autosol. One should keep checking the filling in latter stages by running the fingertips over the surface and by viewing under an oblique light which will show up discrepancies. The most critical examination in the last stages is to apply one thin coat of paint with a spray. This needs only to be a mixture of polyurethane with white pigment thinned down to spraying consistency. One even coat alone need be applied as this will be quite sufficient to show any inaccuracies and one will know then if any refilling or adjustments are required. This is in fact the best way to test a filling since the naked eye cannot always pick up very slight faults and neither can the fingertips. The polyurethane is easily removed with solvent and, before the retouching begins, the filling and surrounding area should be given a final swab over with acetone.

The same Araldite composition is used for filling and making up missing areas in all porcelains, bone china and hard bodied objects and there is no real objection to it being used in a similar manner on some earthenwares where a durable filling is required, but care must be observed to prevent staining, and in general on these more porous bodies Polyfilla is used as the making up composition. Polyfilla, if mixed properly, makes a very strong filling which is easy to build up and also to rub down. For the best results it should be mixed up in the proportions mentioned in the section on materials for filling, but if one remembers that its consistency should be thick like modelling clay rather than wet, then there is no reason for it to be less than successful. As it contains its own adhesive it will bond strongly to the sides of the area to be filled provided that contact is made over the entire area. In the same way as with Araldite, then, it is advisable to smear some of the Polyfilla along the break edges before filling in the aperture.

Sellotape will suffice as a support if one is required, but if the area is not too large the Polyfilla will usually hold its own shape. The filling is applied with a spatula, pressing in well a small portion at a time which will help to exclude air bubbles. Again accuracy at this point will save excess work later. The surface can be smoothed down with a little water on the spatula, the finger or a soft wide paint brush.

If Sellotape has been used at the back as a support, as soon as the filling is hard enough, this should be removed to allow the area to dry out. Depending on the thickness of the filling, the Polyfilla will dry quite quickly, but to be on the safe side it is probably better to leave it a full twenty-four hours. The rubbing down procedure is similar to that with Araldite putty, using abrasive papers and one will almost certainly have to make adjustments by applying more filler where pin holes and blemishes occur. With patient work one can achieve an excellent finish with Polyfilla, but this effort can be considerably reduced now by the introduction of a new grade of Polyfilla especially made for fine surfaces. This is called Fine Surface Polyfilla and is supplied already mixed as as paste for immediate use. In itself it is not suitable to use as a filler, and so the ordinary grade is used as described before except that when it has been rubbed down to near perfection the finer grade is applied over the surface, filling in all the pin holes and blemishes. This is allowed to dry and using a fine grade of abrasive paper the final surface is achieved. Polyfilla closely resembles the texture of earthenware and, if colour is added, the retouching of an object where the colour of the body comes through a fairly transparent glaze is often made easier. The colour of the filler to the object can be matched very accurately but here one gets better with practice, for at first it may be difficult to judge the amount of pigment that will be required. The reason for this is that the Polyfilla will dry several tones lighter than it looks when wet. However, once the correct combination of dry artists' pigments are dispersed evenly into the powder, water is then added and the filler is mixed to a stiff consistency. It will be quite useful to keep back some of the dry powder and pigment mixture for future use in refilling this object and others of similar colouring. This reserve can be kept in a container with the tone indicated. Where one is working on an unglazed earthenware object, and one will almost certainly have to adjust a filling, any discrepancy in colour would matter, and this reserve of the original powder and pigment will be invaluable.

Where the gap to fill is more than an inch in width and height, then the Polyfilla should be built up by degrees. It will hold its shape to a certain extent and where the limit is reached, it should be left to set hard; the next level can then be added on top, and so on until the gap is filled. This way one will acquire a firm nucleus upon which to build up the surface to be uniformly level with its surroundings.

MODELLING

Polyfilla is also an excellent medium to model up with. It can be used for a permanent fixture, or an arm or limb can be modelled up with the Polyfilla and a mould made and then a cast taken in a material such as Araldite.

There are various mediums that one can use for binding up missing parts from which a cast can be made, such as wax, Plasticine, modelling clay and the Polyfilla above, and the choice of which to use lies with the restorer.

In practice though it is usually preferable, and on balance takes no longer, to model straight on to the object with the permanent composition. In the case of porcelains and other hard bodied objects this would be the Araldite compounds, and for terra cottas, earthenwares and for some Parian wares, Polyfilla is suitable. In a museum it is most likely that one will be able to find a pattern from which to work, but in any case, where a missing limb or vital area of an object such as a figurine needs to be made up, one must have, at the very least, a photograph of a similar object to copy from. Missing areas such as this should not be made up unless an accurate record is available for reference. The restorer must be able to model to a very high standard and able to adapt his style to the object upon which he is working. He must be capable of modelling up hands, however small, that are correct in proportion and structure, and resembling perfectly the corresponding hand on the figure. One should not assume that where the modelling on a figure is very simple, e.g. merely giving an indication of bone structure beneath the surface, the task will be any easier. This becomes apparent with Staffordshire pottery, which seems to be very simply and sometimes crudely modelled with just the faintest suggestion of bone structure, but the restorer will probably underestimate the time that it will take to restore hands or arms to the same simplicity and yet be convincing. Another point to remember here is that the surface coating will fill in a lot of detail and also increase the dimensions slightly. Therefore any detail must be overestimated to allow for this, and care must be observed in making sure that the size of the limb is accurate – neither too large nor too small. Callipers will help to make the comparison between the limb being modelled up and the corresponding original. Where a whole or part of a limb is missing a dowel or supporting armature will be needed upon which to build the basic shape. A hole must be drilled into the porcelain and for this a diamond point will be needed. As these points are available down to very small sizes, some of which are illustrated in the section on equipment, there are few occasions where a hole cannot be drilled. However, if it is not possible to drill, then as illustrated in Fig. 10a a block of Araldite putty is applied to the break edge, keeping it within the perimeter of the outline, and when this has begun to set and is in a rubbery state, wires for the fingers can be inserted. Fifteen amp fuse wires can be usefully employed where the fingers are very

Figure 10a

Block of Araldite putty applied to break edge and allowed to semi-set. Wires for fingers then placed in correct position

Dowel hole drilled and stainless steel rod set in position. The rod is cut to a length just below the knuckle

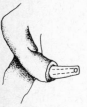

Roughly shaped block of Araldite putty set round dowel. First application allowed to set hard

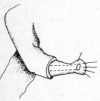

The second layer of Araldite putty applied and allowed to set to a rubbery state. Wires for the fingers then set into position

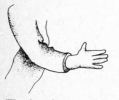

The hand generally modelled up ready for final detail and surfacing

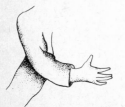

Finished hand ready for retouching

tiny, and will give sufficient support, and for larger dowels, stainless steel or brass is used.

Fig. 10b shows the procedure for building up a hand and part of an arm. In the first illustration the hole has been drilled and the main supporting dowel has been cut to the correct length and set into position with adhesive. The dowel should be deep enough to provide a good anchor for the wire, and of sufficient width to take both the wire and an adhesive or putty with which to bond it strongly in position. Here either Araldite putty mixed to a sticky but firm consistency or Sintolit can be used. The advantage of the Sintolit is that it can be held in place whilst setting, and being well within the perimeter of the outer edge of the porcelain, its discolouration will not matter. One of the fast-setting epoxies could also be used. The Araldite putty, unless the object can be balanced, will probably need a support to prevent the wire from moving out of position whilst setting. The wire rod in the illustration had been cut to just below the level where the knuckle will be, the reason being that one does not want any obstruction to the wires for the fingers which will be positioned later. Once the dowel has set in place, a roughly modelled block of Araldite is applied to the approximate shape of the arm and this will give a solid ground upon which to model. To achieve sufficient bulk for the fingers, probably two applications will be needed as the putty will sag if too much is put on at any one time.

Before this putty has set hard, when in a rubbery state, the finger dowels are inserted into their correct positions. The tips of the dowels which go into the putty should be dipped into neat Araldite before insertion, which will ensure that they will bond strongly. There will be no need for support when the putty is in this condition. Once the composition is set hard, another application of Araldite can be layered on and the fingers approximately shaped in. It is far better to build up patiently in thin layers which will avoid a lot of work rubbing or filing down, particularly on the fingers, which even with supporting dowels are still delicate. As mentioned previously, detail should be slightly overemphasised and can be filed and rubbed down using needle files and wet or dry abrasive paper. A narrow strip of abrasive paper can be drawn up and down between the fingers to smooth the surfaces where it may be difficult to use a file. The joint between the ceramic and the Araldite addition should be absolutely smooth, for when retouched it must be indiscernible and one cannot afford to have any difference in level between the two. Surfacing of the whole made up area can be achieved by first filing down the rougher parts and then using abrasive papers, again remembering that there must be no blemishes which will show up under the retouch.

Building up individual fingers is often required either partially or wholly, and given sufficient area a dowel will help the job considerably. It is possible to build up a finger without a dowel using Araldite putty, since with its such good adhesive properties, unless

46

treated very roughly, Araldite will bond on very strongly. If the break surface is slightly roughened and a small quantity of neat Araldite is applied as a tiny knob one can then build the finger up in degrees with the putty mixture. This may take some time as each application must be allowed to set hard before the next is added. Accuracy is the important factor here too, as one does not want to incur more rubbing down than absolutely necessary. The whole task is obviously much easier if a dowel can be inserted into the break edge of the finger, and this is done as before with a diamond point. Where drilling is concerned, however tiny the hole, one should still be observing the rule to keep both the area being drilled and the drill point cool, carrying out the operation either under water or with a drip. The wire dowel is cut to the correct length, a little shorter than the total length of the finger, and bonded into place with Araldite putty, a fast-setting epoxy or Sintolit (see Fig. 11). It is then modelled up in the same manner as the hand mentioned previously, and surfaced ready for retouching. An alternative method for single fingers can be to mix the Araldite and kaolin to a firm consistency and to roll out a thin rod shape, with its diameter slightly less than the break edge of the original finger. This is then cut to the correct length and placed on silicone paper or polythene and allowed to set hard. If the finger being replaced is crooked or curved, the Araldite putty, when in a semi-set rubbery state can be bent to the correct angle. When fully hardened this can be bonded on to the break edge with neat Araldite. The object will either have to be balanced or Plasticine used as a support to prevent the 'finger' moving before the adhesive has set. This will provide a perfect foundation on which to apply a second layer of putty and shape the correct form of the finger. Finishing off is the same as with previous modelling in this medium.

Missing petals, flowers or leaves are always having to be made up and this can be achieved in a variety of ways. Half petals are usually built up directly on the object using Plasticine as a support, and where there are whole petals missing there are usually others on the object from which to copy. One of the easiest methods is to mix up Araldite, titanium dioxide and kaolin to a stiff putty and to roll it out like pastry on a sheet of glass, using kaolin powder to prevent sticking, to the required thickness. The desired shape is then cut out with a blade, dipped from time to time in methylated spirit to ensure a clean cut edge. Lines and other indentations can be made with a modelling tool and the leaves are then placed on silicone paper to set. If they need to be curved, this can be done when the putty has reached a rubbery stage. The fingers should be dusted with a little kaolin powder before bending the leaves or petals to the desired angle, and any further impressions or lines can be emphasised at this stage. These are left to harden fully and can then be trimmed, fitted and bonded on to the object with 'neat' Araldite.

A strip of putty can be rolled out to a collar shape with the top

Figure 11

Dowel holes drilled and wires in place

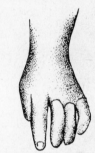

Roughly modelled up with Araldite putty

Finished fingers ready for retouching

47

edge cut with six or so petal shapes, and the whole strip is then rolled up in the fingers. A modelling tool pressed into the centre will open up the petals. Surplus composition underneath which will have elongated when being rolled up, can be cut off if not required. Depending on the petal shape cut on the top edge of the collar, a variety of different flowers can be made this way. Alternatively, individual petals of the same style can be made and allowed to set hard, and these can then be assembled by using a pad of semi-set putty in which to anchor them, either already seated in position on the object, or free standing to be bonded on when the whole unit has set hard.

Press moulds of simply constructed flowers from the same object can be taken with Plasticine or Paribar, which is a dental moulding compound, or with rubber latex and silicone rubber. The two latex materials are discussed in the section on moulding and casting. Obviously these moulding materials can reduce the amount of work, but where they are not convenient or possible to use, the restorer must resort to his own modelling skill with a degree of ingenuity. Where the object is an earthenware, for example a chinese figure or a terra cotta model, then Polyfilla is the most suitable medium to use for building up hands, limbs and other missing areas. As mentioned before, colour can be introduced into the Polyfilla and if the correct tone is achieved it may not always be necessary to retouch, as the surface texture will be very similar. Dowels should be used in the same manner as with the Araldite putty, and although Polyfilla is strong, it will not stand such rigorous filing or rubbing down as the putty, so in most cases individual fingers should have an internal wire support. It should also be built up layer by layer and for finer detail and finish the Fine Surface variety can be used as the last application. To make sure of a good adhesion to the object, a little polyvinyl acetate emulsion can be mixed with the primary application. As with any modelled up area, the final surface is all important and must be perfect to receive the retouch; in the case of Polyfilla this may take a while if the fine surface type is not used, since pin holes are apt to keep appearing – but patience will again win the day.

Using either Araldite putty or Polyfilla one should be able to overcome most modelling and filling problems on ceramics.

CHAPTER NINE
Moulding and Casting

The need to make castings will occur at some time in the restorer's career, for although direct modelling can be employed for most jobs, it can take a painfully long time to achieve a satisfactory result, and where there are a number of identical shapes to reproduce it would be uneconomical to model each one individually. With moulding materials such as rubber latex emulsion and silicone rubber available, making casts is usually a relatively easy process. The latex is the most flexible of the two, and would be used for moulds of hands and intricate shapes rather than the silicone rubber which can tear.

Where there is a missing limb from a figurine to replace one is faced with two possibilities. If there are only photographic records of the complete figure or one similar, then direct modelling is the only answer to the problem; but if there is another identical figure in an undamaged state available, a mould can then be taken from the relevant area, and a cast made to be fitted to the damaged piece. Taking the example of a hand and part of the arm, the moulding material would need to be flexible enough to be peeled off easily in one piece, and for this quality one would use latex emulsion. The arm itself must be cleaned with acetone to remove any dirt or grease that may have accumulated on the surface. A sufficient quantity of latex is put into a small container, with a lid, as it will begin to coagulate on contact with the air. A small jar or yoghurt carton are ideal receptacles. As the latex will ruin brushes, unless one has an old one to hand that is disposable, an orange or cocktail stick with some cotton wool rolled on to the tip makes an ideal applicator. The swab stick is dipped into the latex and a first coating is applied to the arm, making sure that the whole surface is covered, being extra careful in between the fingers to see that air bubbles do not form. Any air bubbles that do occur can be removed by blowing or picking with a pin, for if allowed to remain they will spoil the surface of the mould and will pick up as blemishes on the cast.

Having ensured that this first coating is free from bubbles and covers the entire surface, the object is left until the latex has set. At this stage it will become a transparent light brown and is then ready for the next coat to be applied. The time it takes to set will depend on the temperature in the room; if warm it will take less time, but it is not advisable to place the object on a radiator or in a low oven to speed up setting. This may cause the latex to shrink and pull away, particularly from hollow areas such as between the fingers, causing detail to be lost. The second coat is applied as the first, allowing it to set and the process is repeated until the mould is considered to be of sufficient thickness. For just a hand which is very small, three or four coats will be adequate to form a firm enough mould to take the casting material without distorting. On a hand which is more than half an inch from fingertip to wrist, six or seven coatings will be required. A whole arm will probably require more for it to be rigid enough to prevent it going out of shape when filled, but either way one must keep the coating even and not too thick, remembering that it has to be peeled from the arm down over the wrist, which will be a narrower area than the rest of the arm, and over the fingers. The fingers will be vulnerable and one must avoid snapping them off, which will happen if too much force is needed to peel the latex off. Common sense should tell one when the mould is thick enough.

At least twelve hours should be allowed between application of the last layer of latex and removal of the mould. The outer surface should be dusted thoroughly with French chalk to avoid the rubber sticking to itself as it is rolled back. The mould is then carefully peeled off, easing it gently when one gets to the finger area, and when completely removed, while it is inside out, the interior surface is lightly dusted with French chalk; it is then turned back to its correct shape.

Araldite AY103/HY951 or 956 with titanium dioxide is used for the casting material as it will be liquid enough to pour easily into the tiniest of areas. The white pigment is thoroughly ground into the Araldite in a quantity just sufficient to give a white colour to the resin but not so much as to thicken it. The mixture should be fluid enough to pour under normal conditions, but if it is thought necessary, or where the fingers really are minute, it can be warmed slightly to make it even more liquid. The Araldite is poured into the mould in a thin, steady stream down one side into the mould. For a simple mould, this will ensure that the air is pushed out, but where there are fingers at the bottom one is very likely to get air trapped so it is wise to pour in a small quantity first of all and knead the finger area to ensure that any air is squashed out. Tapping the mould gently on the table top will also help to dislodge bubbles.

50

When satisfied that the fingers are filled, the rest of the resin is poured in slowly until the mould is full. The filled mould is then supported and left until the resin has cured and then the rubber is removed in the same way as for the original arm. The cast is closely examined for any surface blemishes which can be made good with Araldite putty. One is unlikely to get away with a perfect cast as it will either have one or two pin holes or air bubbles that need refilling, or it will require rubbing down where rough patches have occurred. In either case, if the mould was made well, there should be very little work required on the cast. Having got the surface of the cast into a perfect condition, the limb will probably need to be trimmed down where it is to be joined on to the figure. This is done by filing and rubbing down until one gets a perfect union between the two surfaces. Depending on the object, the limb can either be dowelled on to the figure, or just bonded on with Araldite.

Th latex emulsion can also be used for making a mould for filling in missing areas on rims of plates, bowls, vases or anywhere that the area is too large to be filled without a support. In order to make the latex rigid enough for this type of mould, cotton flock or fine sawdust can be mixed in until the latex is of paste consistency. When set, this will still be flexible enough to remove easily, but will hold its shape firmly when placing over the missing area to be filled. The mould is taken from an area on the plate which is intact, and if there is a raised pattern which may be repetitive, one must make sure that the mould is made on an area of the pattern which will correspond to the gap which is being filled. Latex by itself is painted on the surface of the china in the first instance to ensure total coverage and the exclusion of air bubbles. Cotton flock or sawdust is mixed into the remaining latex to make a paste consistency that will hold its position when applied. This is then laid on to the pre-coated surface with a spatula or palette knife to an even thickness of between $\frac{1}{8}$ to $\frac{1}{4}$in., depending on the size of the aperture. One must make sure that the size of the mould will be adequate to cover the missing area plus a surrounding margin of at least $\frac{1}{4}$in. The latex should also be taken right up to the top of the rim and overlapped a little to the other side, in the same way that Plasticine and Paribar are used for press moulds. The flock and latex mixture will take up to twenty-four hours to cure, depending on its thickness and should not be removed until it has taken on a brown colour.

If one is making a large mould, possibly taken on a curve where one may have doubts about it holding its shape, a plaster of Paris casing or outer mould can be applied on top of the rubber to ensure rigidity, but this must not be added until the latex has fully cured. The mould is removed and placed in position over the area to be filled and can be held in position if necessary with a strip or two of Sellotape. If a plaster casing has been made, the plate will most likely have to be supported at a slight angle or wedged from beneath, as it may be a little top heavy. The same Araldite with

51

Figure 12

white pigment is mixed up, and a little is painted round the break edges to provide a good bond; it is also wise to apply one coat on to the surface of the mould which will ensure total surface coverage and that there will be no air bubbles. The remainder of the Araldite and white pigment is mixed with kaolin to produce a putty-like consistency, and this is then layered into the mould with a spatula. It must be well pressed down and it is better to add it little by little rather than in one lump. The surface can be smoothed down with the spatula dipped in a little methylated spirit. When set, the mould is peeled off and any discrepancies are corrected either by adding more putty or rubbing down until the filling is ready for retouching.

One is always coming across the need to replace flowers and leaves, and this job will be much easier if moulds can be taken from other complete flowers on the object. Any very deep undercuts should be filled in with Plasticine first to prevent the rubber getting trapped. The surface of the flower is cleaned with acetone and the latex is applied either layer by layer, slightly overlapping the edges of the petals, or one can pre-coat the flower with neat latex and then add a coating of latex and cotton flock mixed to a paste. It is a very good idea to build up a collection of moulds and casts of flowers, hands, etc., as they can come in very useful (see Fig. 12). These moulds can be made very easily and a reserve consisting of many different varieties of cast flowers and leaves can save a great deal of time.

As mentioned in the section on modelling, Plasticine or Paribar press moulds can be made from simply constructed flowers where there is little undercut. Time can be saved using these materials since one does not have to wait for the mould to cure as one would with latex. Similarly one can also use silicone rubber which sets in about

52

half an hour. This rubber is nowhere near as flexible as the latex, but it is quite suitable for making moulds of items that have no deep undercuts where the rubber is likely to get caught. The grade of silicone rubber most commonly used is Silastomer 9161 with a catalyst No. N9162 mixed in the ratio of 4 per cent catalyst to rubber. This rubber is quite fluid but one can use it in the same way as the latex by applying one thin coat, and then adding a mixture of rubber with enough cotton flock to give it substance and to prevent it from running down a sloping surface. Alternatively, having blocked deep undercuts with Plasticine, one can build a wall round the flower or whatever with more Plasticine and then pour the neat rubber in. This will set in half an hour and when the wall is removed, the mould is eased off the flower and filled with Araldite and white pigment. Silicone rubber moulds should always be further cured in the oven for one hour at $100^{\circ}C$ before filling as this will prevent epoxy resins sticking to and spoiling the mould which can happen if this precaution is not taken. Silastomer silicone rubber can also be used for making moulds for plate rims or any area where detail does not go so deep that there is a likelihood of it tearing on removal. Its advantage of quick setting can often make up for its lack of flexibility. Both Silastomer and latex will be suitable to use for a plate which is of an open-worked design where casting the missing area will be far quicker and easier than modelling up free-hand. The mould must be taken from an area on the rim which will exactly correspond with the missing gap, and is normally applied on the top side of the plate rim as this is where the most detail will be.

To prevent the rubber from going too far through the holes in the lattice-work, a layer of Plasticine is placed across the underside of the plate rim. If using latex, this is applied in the usual manner with a pre-coating, followed by a latex and cotton flock paste, making sure that the holes are filled properly; it is then left to cure fully. With Silastomer, either cotton flock can be added, or again a Plasticine wall can be built round the area which will contain the rubber when poured in. In the latter case it will probably be necessary to bed the plate rim down on to a block of Plasticine, so that it is resting in a horizontal position and the rubber will retain a level when poured. One must make sure that the area walled off for the mould is large enough, and allows room for sufficient overlap round the gap in the plate rim to be filled. The rubber is poured in to a depth of about a quarter of an inch or more depending on the size of the mould. This is then allowed to set, and when removed, the mould is further cured in the oven and dusted with French chalk. The mould, whether latex or Silastomer, is then placed in its correct position over the gap, making sure that the design of the lattice work in the mould links up with the break edges on the rim. The mould can be taped or wedged to ensure that it fits tightly and does not move. The Araldite AY103/HY951 or 956 is mixed with a little white pigment, some of which is smeared on to the break edges of the china and also painted over the surface of the mould. The remainder is mixed to a putty consistency with kaolin, which is pressed in with a spatula and then allowed to set hard.

The mould is removed carefully and in the case of the Silastomer, it must be pulled away gently or it may tear. The cast area is trimmed, refilled or rubbed down if necessary and then finally surfaced for retouching. There should be no blemishes or discernible surface differences between the filling and the original, particularly at the joint areas.

Two-piece moulds can be made with the latex rubber, and this will be useful for cup or other handles which would be impossible to get out of a one-piece mould without having to cut it. This process is described more fully with the aid of a series of photographs in the section on 'Making a cast of a cup handle' (see p. 77).

CHAPTER TEN
Retouching

This is the last process in ceramic restoration and is almost certainly the most difficult. Its success depends on the quality of all the work carried out in the previous steps. Retouching will not cover up any mistakes, it will in fact reveal them and thus the perfection of the surface to be painted is all important.

It is virtually impossible to describe how one achieves perfection in retouching as this does depend entirely on the skills of the restorer. One does not always necessarily have to aim for an invisible retouch, but one that is acceptable to the eye. In the case of museum objects, the latter is usually preferred, mainly due to the fact that an invisible retouch nearly always means that the painting has been carried beyond the repaired area, whether to a lesser or greater degree. It is all too easy to carry the paint over a wider area than necessary, perhaps to a convenient part of the ceramic where it changes colour or a contour where the paint can be easily tailed off. This should never be done unless the owner of the object desperately wants an invisible repair and is fully aware of the fact that the retouching will be extended over the glaze.

MATERIALS REQUIRED
Materials and methods for retouching also vary considerably, but whatever medium or method one uses, a great deal of patience and skill will be needed. No two restorers are likely to use the same procedure even if they employ the same materials, so the individual must follow the route that he or she finds most suitable.

The retouching medium itself needs to be clear, as non-discolouring as possible, to dry hard enough to rub down and polish, and also to be easy to apply. Most media will discolour eventually, some far quicker than others, so the choice is difficult. Stoving enamels possess most of the qualities needed but their main disadvantage is that they are heat curing and any object will be subjected to temperatures 150°F at least three times and possibly as much as six. On some objects this can cause damage to the glaze so one must observe discretion if it is going to be used. For domestic wares it may be the most suitable medium as it will stand up to hot water and further heating, but even so a cold curing medium such as polyurethane will achieve comparable results. There are several stoving enamels on the market including Paralac made by ICI and Chintex, the latter being the easiest to obtain in small quantities. All require stoving at up to 350°F for about forty minutes between each stage of painting and for an hour for the final surface coating. A temperature of around 220°F will be sufficient for Chintex. Oil colours will mix in with the Chintex but good quality artist's dry pigments are far superior. For a cold curing medium, which is preferable to any stoving enamel, a polyurethane will offer most of the requirements, being very hard, durable and easy to use. Again there are many such varnishes available and the most suitable is PU 11, made by Furniglas. The best alternative to the PU 11, if there is any difficulty in acquiring it, would be Rustins clear gloss, which although it is a darker colour to start with appears not to discolour as quickly or badly as some other brands. The PU 11 is a very pale yellow, is virtually non-discolouring and is of the right consistency to be used with ease either by brushing or in a spray gun.

It is always better to decant the required amount from the can to a glass tube or pot, with a lid or cover, and use as needed from there rather than from the original container. Polyurethanes set on contact with the air and if the lid is left off the can for any length of time a skin will form on the surface and all will be lost. By decanting and always making sure that the lid has been replaced tightly, the bulk of the polyurethane will keep for much longer.

One can achieve as good a result with polyurethane as with a stoving enamel, and so it is really quite unnecessary to subject any object to heating at all.

Other materials that will be required for retouching include a full range of artists' dry pigments of the best quality. These are finely ground and easily mixed into any medium. They are obtainable in ounce quantities from either Winsor and Newton or Robersons or through any good artists' materials shop, and as they are mostly very strong colours, an ounce of each will last for a long time. It would be more economical to buy titanium dioxide white pigment in a larger quantity as it is used for other processes besides retouching.

The following list of pigments should provide all the colours that will be needed, either by themselves or in combination with each other.

WHITE   Titanium dioxide
BLACK   Lamp and Loory black
BLUES   Cobalt blue; French ultramarine; Prussian blue

GREENS	Viridian or Monastral; terre verte
BROWNS	Burnt umber; raw umber
REDS	Burnt sienna; light red; Alizarin crimson; cadmium red or vermilion
YELLOWS	Yellow ochre; raw Sienna; chrome yellow; lemon yellow; chrome orange

The solvents required will be white spirit for the Rustins polyurethane and a cellulose thinner such as Gipgloss for the PU 11. Most stoving enamels will also need a cellulose thinner, but Chintex Clear Glaze has its own thinner. Brushes must be good quality sable hair and the sizes are selected for the job in hand. One will find that sizes between 00 and 2 will cover most needs. They must be well looked after and cleaned thoroughly after each use; store them in a drawer box where they will not pick up dust or dirt.

For mixing pigments with the medium one will need a suitably sized palette knife, preferably of stainless steel and a reasonably large palette. One can either buy a white palette from an artist's shop or make one from a sheet of white formica. Off-cuts of formica are easily obtainable quite cheaply from do-it-yourself shops.

For gilding one can use either gold leaf in transfer form or gold tablet. The latter is a gold powder bond in gum arabic and soluble in water; it is applied with a brush and when set can be lightly burnished with an agate resulting in an excellent finish. It is relatively expensive for the amount one gets, but as it is usually only used for small areas it is surprising how long it will last. As it is easy to apply and the results are good it is definitely worth investing in. Most good art shops such as Winsor and Newton have it in stock, though it is more economical to purchase it directly from George Whiley Ltd in Ruislip – as is the gold leaf. The full address is supplied in the materials list.

Gold leaf is far more manageable if bought in transfer form. In this form the film of gold is attached to fine tissue paper sheets and one can cut strips of the required size to lay down without the chance of the leaf curling up or being blown away. Loose gold powder is extremely expensive and does not exactly have any advantage over the tablet form. There are also gold preparations on the market such as treasure gold or Liquid Leaf, the latter being extremely useful for intricate patterns that need to be retouched as it paints on very easily. It is available in about twelve different shades including silver and pewter, but unfortunately does not have the lustre of either the tablet or leaf gold and its stability is not guaranteed. Bronze powders can be used but unless they are very finely ground one cannot easily get a smooth uniform surface when mixed with a medium. They will also turn black eventually due to oxidisation in the atmosphere, and the only way this can be prevented is always to bind the powder thoroughly in a medium such as polyurethane and apply a protective coating on top.

These powders are obtainable in various shades, and if bought in a superfine grade can be usefully employed for imitating a lustre glaze. A combination of tones, possibly with a little aluminium powder well bound in the polyurethane medium, can provide an iridescent film, either applied over or under a colour. Obviously one would have to experiment to find out if the metallic film should be laid down first and a transparent colour applied on top, or if a better result can be achieved by carrying out the process the other way round.

APPLYING AND MIXING COLOURS

With all retouching a certain amount of experimentation with colours is definitely not a waste of time. Unless one really knows each colour and what its possibilities are either by itself or in combination with one or more other pigments, a great deal of time can be spent just matching one colour. There are no rules that can be set down as to which colours used in combination will achieve any one specific tone, as this you will learn mainly by trial and error. A white glaze, for instance, cannot be retouched with white pigment alone. You will find that it has either a warm or cool tone, and other pigments such as brown or yellow ochre will have to be added to achieve the warm tone, and at the opposite end of the scale, blues or greens for the cool tones. For this reason, it can sometimes be easier to give the area to be retouched a preliminary coat of white pigment, and comparing this against the surrounding glaze one can decide from which combination of pigments the correct tone can be achieved. This will probably apply only to the glazes which are slightly off-white and are naturally difficult to match. For a glaze of a much stronger tone, such as the blue-green background one finds on Chinese ceramics, a base tone can already have been prepared within the filling as described in the section on retouching, and this will often prove very helpful in obtaining a final match.

In general, the principles for applying paint are more or less the same whether using a stoving enamel or a cold curing polyurethane, and in both cases before application, the surface of the filling must be thoroughly degreased and made free from any dust particles or hair. The brush and palette must also be impeccably clean as any dust particles will seriously impair the smooth application of paint.

The dry pigments are selected and a small quantity of each is put on to a separate surface other than the palette where the mixing will take place. An ordinary tile or sheet of glass will be suitable, and the reason for keeping the pigments separate is that being very light they can easily be blown by a draught or the breath and one does not want stray particles getting into the mixed medium and spoiling the tone. The required amount of polyurethane PU 11 is taken from the tube and put on the palette and into this pigment is mixed with either a spatula or palette knife. It must be remembered that although these pigments are already fine, they still need to be well ground into the medium. The pigment should be ground into a

58

small amount of PU 11 at first and the amount of medium can then be increased to get the right transparency or density. This will be easier than trying to mix a large amount at once. It may also be more helpful to mix the colours with the medium in separate units before continuing to work them as this enables one to judge the strength of each pigment and the amount that will be needed to obtain the correct density and tone. All pigments, especially titanium dioxide, should be so well ground in that there are no particles left and the mixture is absolutely smooth. Some of the pigments are coarser than others and will need more grinding, others may be fine enough to dispense easily with a brush, and these differences will become apparent with use. Even dispersion is essential as the colours may tend to separate out from each other if more than one or two are mixed together and the retouch will be streaky. In all cases the colur mixed on the palette will dry out slightly darker, so one must allow for this when applying the paint to the ceramic. The preliminary coat of paint should be mixed to a much lighter tone than will be required and the subsequent layers can then be adjusted until the correct colour matching is achieved.

Having degreased the surface of the filling and mixed the PU 11 and pigment to the required base tone, this first coat is applied evenly on to the area up to the edge of the repair and then left to set hard for at least twenty-four hours. This layer of paint will probably have quite a matt finish due to the amount of pigment, but this will be of no consequence as there will be at least two or three more layers to be added. If the surface, when set, is not completely smooth, which is generally the case, it is gently rubbed down with a very fine abrasive paper or Flex-i-grit to prepare it for the next application.

The second coating will be aimed more at matching the ultimate colour and will be more transparent, or certainly the ratio of pigment to the polyurethane will be less than it was for the first application. The PU 11 can be thinned a little if required, which will make it less likely to form a ridge at the edge and enable it to be drawn out thinly to the surrounding glaze. If several layers are likely to be required, then thinning the PU 11 will probably be necessary, but one must be careful not to over dilute or the surface will become matt and lose some of its hardness. Each application of paint must be allowed to dry thoroughly and be rubbed down before the next layer is added. If one is using a stoving enamel the same principles apply, but heat is used to cure each layer in accordance with the type of stoving enamel employed. One important point is never to take the object out of the oven whilst it is still hot, otherwise it could easily crack on contact with cold air. It is safer to turn the oven off and leave the object inside until the temperature has dropped right down to normal.

The merging of the painted area with the surrounding glaze is a very difficult process. There will probably tend to be a slight ridge where the applied paint stops at the edge of the filling and this has to be drawn outwards with a fine brush using a series of short strokes. If the paint layer has started to become slightly tacky this will not be easy, but if the brush is dipped into solvent, just sufficient to damp the top of the bristles, this will enable the PU 11 to be feathered out. The paint layer should only overlap on to the surrounding glaze by the minutest margin.

One may have to apply as many as six layers of paint, each one being allowed to set hard and then rubbed down so that finally there is no discrepancy between the retouched area and the surrounding glaze either in colour or surface quality. Obviously each layer must be rubbed down to a certain extent, or one will end up with a lump where the retouch is, but if care is taken to apply each layer evenly and not too thickly, avoiding brush strokes, this rubbing down will be minimal. The last coating should have only a small quantity of pigment mixed in, and if the colour, whether opaque or transparent, has been carefully built up to a perfect match, it can virtually be a clear coat. The polyurethane has in itself a sufficiently gloss finish, and if not overloaded with pigment it will retain this quality, which means that a surface coating as such is not always necessary. The retouch can be given a final polish with Solvol Autosol if after the last application any slight surface discrepancies remain. For a matt finish which will be required for Wedgwood or Parian ware, a matting agent such as TK 800 or HK 125 can be added into the PU 11 either before or after mixing. These particular matting agents are obtainable from a London firm, but others are available through a museum supplier and the addresses of both are supplied in the materials list. The TK 800 is for unpigmented lacquers and the HK 125 is for pigmented lacquers and the degree of mattness depends on the quality of agent added.

Decoration and detail are not usually added until after the second or third layer of paint has been applied and already matches the background glaze of the ceramic. This decoration may be in the form of a repetitive pattern to a border or other designs such as flowers, animals, leaves, etc., and in the case of the latter one must adapt one's painting style to that of the style used for the original designs. Border patterns are often simple and can be applied free-hand, but if of a very symmetrical nature it may be just as well to mark out the points where it repeats itself as a guide. As colours on ceramic glazes are rarely completely opaque, apart from the obvious exceptions of Parian ware or Wedgwood, etc., even the densest of colours such as blue will have a certain transparency. A turquoise colour which may appear opaque is often deceiving. The basic one or two coats will probably be mixed with a certain amount of white pigment, but it will be found that subsequent layers of paint leading up to the final surface will be transparent in order to obtain the correct tonal effect.

For brilliant but dense colours such as blues and greens, it is often better to have a pure white base which will penetrate through the ensuing transparent overtones of colour. As mentioned previously with white glazes, these other purer colours will also possess either warm or cool tonal quality. This applies particularly to blue where one has a dark colour with a slight warm, purple tint such as found continually on Worcester porcelain; this can be imitated using French ultramarine with a little alizarin crimson mixed in to give the warm tone. For a cooler blue such as seen on Chinese porcelain and some Delft ware, a cobalt blue would be used for the basic colour with either a little black, brown or green added. One can achieve a relatively cool colour with ultramarine by mixing in greens, browns or black, but one cannot successfully achieve a warm tone with cobalt blue. Any red mixed with this shade of blue will tend to produce a rather muddy result. Blues in particular behave rather strangely under different light, for example fluorescent lighting will bring out a definite purple tone in ultramarine, so care must be taken for final retouching surfaces to be completed under whichever lighting conditions the object is likely to be displayed.

Greens of all shades can be achieved by mixing blues and yellows together plus sometimes a third pigment to obtain the warm or cool tone. Viridian green is a useful pigment and can be mixed with a variety of other colours to reproduce either transparent or opaque tones. Alizarin crimson as mentioned, in combination with ultramarine blue, will give a warm purple tint, and this crimson with light red and a suspicion of cobalt blue matches the red found on Delft ware. If a brighter red is required to imitate the colour commonly found on a lot of oriental porcelain, the combination of cadmiun red and burnt sienna, and for darker tones a little burnt umber, will provide an excellent match.

One could go on with suggestions, but every restorer will have his own methods and ideas on matching and applying colours; once one has become familiar with the individual colours and their possibilities, this task will become gradually easier and one will be able to match the colours almost by instinct.

SPRAYING

Most retouching can be achieved by using just the brush to apply the paint, but a spray gun can be extremely useful where there is a relatively large background area to retouch and even if there is decoration to be applied on top, it may be too great an area to achieve a uniform surface with the brush and possibly too difficult to tail off the retouch to invisibility. This can be particularly laborious on a single coloured object, but with a spray gun the colour will be laid on evenly with a little edge to the paint. A final surface coating can also be applied with a spray gun either with a little pigment added or as a clear glaze. Although the spray gun has obvious advantages, such as speed, it should not be solely relied upon for retouching, for the paint is certainly liable to encroach over the edge of the repair on to the glaze and without due care one can end up with an overlap of half an inch without realising it. Obliterating a crack by spraying may appear an easy and quick solution but this could also result in a band of paint up to an inch wide, which would not be acceptable. It would be far better to make sure that all dirt and stain has been removed from these cracks in the initial stages of the restoration process and then retouching would not be necessary.

The polyurethane PU 11 can be sprayed successfully as can most stoving enamels, but it has to be thinned considerably to a consistency suitable to go through the nozzle of the spray gun. This will probably be around an equal amount of thinners to the PU 11 or other medium. The required colour is mixed into the polyurethane on the palette, then tipped into the cup of the spray gun and the thinner is added little by little until the correct consistency is achieved. At the same time the pressure is tested and adjusted until the paint is spraying evenly without splattering or 'orange-peeling'. The latter will probably mean that either the gun is being held too close to the surface of the ceramic, or the air pressure is too high, or the mixture may be too thin. Splattering would be due either to the mixture being too thick, which can be easily remedied by adding more thinner, or to the fact that the pigment has not been ground into the medium well enough and odd particles are intermittently blocking the nozzle causing the gun to spit. In the latter case, the gun must be emptied out and cleaned through with solvent, and the pigment and medium remixed, this time with more care. When all these problems have been sorted out and the correct consistency and pressure have been found, the paint can be sprayed on to the required area. To achieve a uniform surface, the paint is sprayed on in a series of parallel lines, slightly overlapping, with the gun either moving back and front along the width of the repair, or in a circular movement, making sure that the gun is continually travelling over the surface to prevent the paint being concentrated in any one place. It will be necessary for more than one or two layers to be applied, and each must be allowed to set hard before the next is applied, rubbing down in between if required in the same manner as with a brush retouch. It is possible to regulate the size of the spray on most guns from a wide down to a very narrow line, and it is therefore wise to close down the aperture when spraying along the edge of the repaired area, thus minimising the amount of paint that might travel on to the surrounding glaze.

Various effects can be achieved with a spray gun such as speckling and shading. For the first, one holds the gun further away from the job than usual and larger spots can be obtained by lowering the pressure. Shading is easily achieved by spraying the denser colour normally and where the tone becomes lighter the gun is drawn away from the object, thus reducing the density of the colour.

Obviously the further the gun is held away from the object the wider the area of sprayed paint that will overlap on to the glaze. All these effects must be practised and experimented with in advance either by using the spray gun or with an ordinary paint brush or a combination of both.

No colouring medium should ever be left in the spray gun after use. It should be tipped out of the cup and the residue flushed through the gun with plenty of solvent. The nozzles are so fine that they can block very easily and one can spend unnecessary time and energy cleaning them out the next day. Brushes should always be cleaned out immediately after use as they are too expensive to ruin, especially if they have only been used once. Any remaining colouring medium should be cleaned off the palette with solvent before it starts to set hard, as the job will be easy at this stage but not so the following day.

LUSTRES AND GILDING

The subject of lustres was mentioned briefly earlier in connection with bronze powders which can be fairly successfully employed. To achieve a lustre effect is probably the most difficult part of the retouching and is still to a certain extent unsolved. However, there is an American firm which produces reflective colours for obtaining lustrous effects; these are being experimented with, and up to the present their possibilities seem to be encouraging. These colours are called Murano Colours (the address of the London agent is given in the materials list and they will probably supply a leaflet on request). There are several shades of lustre available giving blue, pink, green and yellow effects. These used in combination with other pigments will produce various iridescent films. A basically pink lustre film, if the light hits it from another angle, will take on a blue colour and a yellowish film painted on to a light brown base colour will produce a warm iridescent effect often found on lustre glazes. To achieve the required effect a great deal of experimenting with these colours has to be carried out first to find out which films produce the correct shade of lustre and what tone the base colour should be. The Murano colour can be applied by brush or spray, and is mixed into a medium such as polyurethane making sure that it is evenly dispersed. Pigment can also be added at the same time, but the resultant finish is generally more successful if the Murano colour and clear polyurethane are applied as a top surface.

GILDING

Applying gold will be the last step in the retouching process and as one is usually only involved with gilding small areas, transfer gold leaf or tablet gold are the most readily available materials to use. Transfer gold is bought in a book of twenty-five sheets with each film of gold backed by acid-free tissue paper. This makes it easy to handle and small pieces or strips can be cut off with scissors to the approximate size required. There are different shades available: the red gold will match the darker shades and the yellower 24 carat gold will match the most common shade of gilding on most ceramics. For silver decoration, silver leaf is available but possibly white gold leaf may give the better effect.

The surface to be gilded must be absolutely clean, and free from grease and dust, etc. There are many gold sizes to choose from but the polyurethane PU 11 which is used for retouching will be extremely suitable to use. If a stoving enamel has been used for retouching, Chintex for example, this again can be used as a gold size but will have to be stoved in the usual manner. The PU 11 or other medium is painted on to the area evenly, avoiding brush strokes. If applied in too thick a layer, when the gold is laid on it will pick up the shape of brush strokes and have a lumpy and clumsy appearance. If joining up a pattern, the varnish can be carried over a fraction on to the gilding on the china. The gold leaf will attach itself wherever the size medium has been painted, and as this may be difficult to see because of its transparency, a little pigment such as red can be added to the medium so that one can see where the lines or patterns have been painted in. The medium must then be left to reach a slightly tacky state before the leaf is applied. With a stoving enamel such as Chintex this will take about half an hour, and the PU 11 will take a little less, probably nearer fifteen minutes. The transfer gold is cut to a strip of convenient size and is laid on to the prepared surface, gold side down, and the back of the tissue is gently rubbed with the finger. When the tissue is raised, the gold should be lying on the repair in the shape of the pattern and if any gaps are left another strip of gold can be applied straight away. The edges of the pattern will probably be furred due to loose gold, and this can be gently removed by dusting with a soft paintbrush and the loose particles will come away leaving a clean edge. If there are still areas which have not picked up the gold, this will mean that the size was not applied evenly over the whole surface to be gilded. One must allow the first application to dry thoroughly for at least twenty-four hours, and if a stoving enamel was used then the object must be stoved as usual. It is not possible to touch up bare patches so the entire process must be repeated, and in some cases this will often improve the result giving the gold a richer appearance. Burnishing should not be attempted until the medium has had plenty of time to harden, and in the case of gold leaf this will probably not be necessary.

As an alternative to gold leaf, the tablet gold mentioned earlier is fairly easy to apply and will also provide an excellent result. It may be preferable to the gold leaf where the gilding on the china has more of a brassy finish. The tablet gold is painted on with a fine brush which has first been dipped in water and then loaded with the gold. Too much water should not be used or the gold powder will be unevenly dispersed and not lie on the surface. With the fully loaded brush the most successful method is to use a dotting action rather than a stroke, and this will ensure that the gold will cover the required area. The object should then be left for twenty-four hours before burnishing with an agate burnisher. The final result will be a little more brilliant than the finish of gold leaf. The brush that has been used should not be cleaned out as it will still contain a lot of gold powder and can be employed again at a later date, for dipping in water will render it re-usable. Gold in tablet form is expensive and one cannot afford to waste it.

CHAPTER ELEVEN
Problems that may occur

Ceramic restoration is never quite so straightforward as it may seem and one may often come across the odd problem that one has not met before.

FLAKING GLAZE
One such problem could be with an object where the glaze is loose and flaking, or where salts are growing and in many cases where both are happening to the object at once. Flaking of a glaze is often caused by the expansion of salts which have been absorbed into the body of the ceramic, or where an object had been out of doors, got wet and then had been subjected to frost. These problems will usually occur on objects that are earthenware where the body is porous.

Objects that tend to suffer from flaking and salts are very often tiles which at some time have been exposed to the elements and without warning or for any apparent reason, start growing salt crystals which can damage the glaze (see Fig. 13).

Before attempting to consolidate any glaze that may be loose, the offending salts must be removed. These salts will generally be water soluble and can be extracted by immersing the object in de-ionised water. This may sound simple, but one must be extremely careful when doing this not to dislodge any further flakes. Taking a tile as an example, this is placed in an empty polythene or stainless steel tray. De-ionised or distilled water is poured in, but only a very small quantity at first which is allowed to be absorbed gradually by the tile. Then more is added slowly until the level of the water in the container is just below the surface of the glaze. Do not cover the tile with water. By adding water slowly, air in the ceramic body is allowed to escape gradually instead of being suddenly forced out taking the loose flakes with it, and this would happen if the object was plunged straight into water. The water in the tray is changed every day until all the salts are removed. In order to tell when this occurs, a sample of the water is evaporated off, and when there are no salts left in the bottom of the crucible, the tile can be taken out and allowed to dry. It should be left to dry out naturally for several days and no attempt should be made to speed this up by putting the object in an oven.

Consolidation is the next step and for this a polyvinyl acetate solution is used. The strength of the solution depends on such factors as the density of the object and the degree of penetration required. The solution is made up by dissolving chips or beads of polyvinyl acetate solid (Rhodopas B) in 90 per cent acetone and 10 per cent ethyl acetate to form a strong syrupy solution which can be diluted as desired with Cellosolve (2-ethoxy-ethanol). This solvent will give the solution greater penetrating power, and a 2 to 5 per cent solution will probably be a satisfactory strength to use. The object can be placed in a tray and the solution added slowly, being absorbed into the body of the tile by degrees, or it can be applied by brush. When fully impregnated with the solution, the loose flakes can be gently pressed into position.

Figure 13

67

Polyvinyl acetate solution will slightly alter the tonal quality of the object, and if this is totally unacceptable, a polyvinyl alcohol solution should be used as an alternative. This is made up by simply dissolving the PV alcohol powder in warm water until the desired strength is reached. The solution is then strained to remove any lumps and is used in exactly the same way as the polyvinyl acetate solution. On an object just suffering from loose glaze, the polyvinyl acetate or alcohol solution applied with a brush or stick to the local areas will be strong enough to hold the flakes down and prevent further damage.

SPRINGING

Any object that has been fired at a fairly high temperature will be under a certain amount of stress. When this object is broken, particularly if a plate or bowl, the tensions will be released and distortion can occur to one or more of the pieces; this is termed springing. Taking a plate broken in half as an example, one may find that for half the length of the break edge a perfect union can be obtained, but the remainder will be stepped and not fit into place under normal pressure. In some cases it is possible to overcome this problem by strapping very tightly with Sellotape following the usual procedure, but the problems start when either one end will form a perfect alignment or the other, but not both simultaneously. One will either have to compromise and accept the best possible solution under the circumstances or another method can be tried, there being no guarantee that it will be entirely successful. The procedure is as follows.

The adhesive, such as Araldite AY103/HY956, is applied to half the length of the break edge only and the two halves are strapped tightly together, treating the end of the plate with no adhesive in exactly the same way as the end with the adhesive. The reason for this is that the tensioning with the tape must be kept even over the whole plate, otherwise it may move more out of alignment whilst setting if applied unevenly. One must keep checking the joint to be sure that the half with the adhesive is perfectly tight and level. This is then left for the Araldite to cure fully, if possible for two days, when the tape is removed. More adhesive is introduced into the unbonded end of the break, and this is where the process starts to get difficult. Place a strip of folded back Sellotape on one side of the break, and with the fingers carefully press the half of the plate that is raised, down to the level of the other half, at the same time quickly pulling the tape across the break to hold the two halves level. Another strip of tape should be pulled across the back to even the tension. More tape is applied in a systematic manner, back and front, pulling very tightly indeed to prevent the two halves moving out of line.

This method to remedy springing may or may not be successful, but in many cases one can certainly improve on what would otherwise have been a poor alignment. Due care must be observed when trying this method though, as if too much pressure or force is used the plate may end up in three pieces rather than the original two. Common sense must prevail when deciding whether it is possible to pull and press the two sides together without subjecting the plate to overstrain, or whether a compromise must be accepted.

REMOVAL OF ENCRUSTATION

Calcium carbonate encrustation on an object can be removed successfully with hydrochloric acid. A fifty-fifty solution of acid and water will probably suffice, but if necessary the amount of acid to water can be increased. One should be extremely careful when using any acids. Skin and clothing should be protected and the operation should be carried out where no damage can be caused to any other object or persons. A large enough container should be used, placed in a sink preferably of stainless steel, allowing plenty of room so as not to be cramped during the operation. When making up the solution, remember that acid should always be added to water, and never the other way round. The object is presoaked in water and the acid solution then applied on cotton wool held in tweezers or swab sticks. On contact with the calcium carbonate the acid will cause a great deal of fizzing, and when after the first application this dies down, more is added. The object is periodically washed off with water and the process repeated until all the encrustation has been dissolved. After a final good wash the object is allowed to dry out thoroughly.

CHAPTER TWELVE
Objects other than Ceramics

In this chapter materials for restoring objects other than ceramics are discussed. These include glass, jade and ivory which may crop up from time to time and although these are borderline objects for the ceramic restorer, minor repairs can be carried out if one is aware of the correct materials to use. A warning here is that if one is at all doubtful about restoring an object made of an unfamiliar material, expert advice should always be sought before any action is taken.

GLASS
There is no way of disguising breaks in glass as there would be with a ceramic object, and the best one can hope for is to piece the object together so that it is in a relatively safe condition. Glass is a very difficult material to repair mainly because the break edges are extremely smooth and offer little key for the adhesive, and there are few occasions where one can grind the edges to offer some assistance. Glass should never be subjected to heat of any form as it can be easily damaged and could craze. An Araldite adhesive is the most suitable to use for bonding, being by far the strongest available, and as the layer of adhesive between the break edges will be very thin any discolouration will be visibly negligible. All breaks should be thoroughly cleaned with acetone, and if the area allows they can be scored lightly with a diamond-tipped drill to offer some key for the adhesive.

The Araldite is applied to one side of the break and the two pieces are put together using Sellotape to prevent them from slipping before the Araldite sets. It would be very difficult to put an object broken in many pieces together at one attempt, so one must observe all the precautions mentioned in the section on bonding, and make sure that alignment is absolutely perfect on all sections being left to set before the whole is assembled. In the case of a broken stem of a fairly small diameter that would not allow room for a dowel, if the two break edges are lightly scored with a diamond point they should hold together well with Araldite. One must be very careful not to allow the drill point too near the perimeter of the break, or chips of glass may be sheared off thus spoiling the joint.

If the stem is wide enough, a dowel, itself made of glass, will help to make a very strong bond. The two halves of the stem are drilled in the same way as a ceramic, keeping cool with water. Just under or around an eighth of an inch will be deep enough for each dowel hole and the diameter will depend on the size of the stem. A piece of glass rod will serve as a dowel, and this can be bought in various sizes from a laboratory equipment supplier. Depending on the diameter of the drilled hole, this rod may need to be ground down a little in order to fit and this can be done with a diamond drill under water. The correct length is then cut off with a diamond disc. Araldite adhesive is used for bonding and a little is placed in each hole and smeared round. By doing this the ground surface will take on a transparent appearance again. More Araldite is then added to the break surface of one half, the glass dowel is inserted and the two halves of the glass are joined so that they are perfectly aligned. The object will have to be supported while the Araldite sets, for although the dowel will hold the stem quite firmly it could slide slightly off true. Strips of Sellotape from the bowl of the glass to the base or wedges of Plasticine will prevent any chance of the stem moving out of line. In some cases it may be better to up-end the glass and stand it on its rim leaving it to set that way, again using strips of tape as a precaution against the joint moving.

Polyvinyl acetate emulsion can be a very good adhesive for glass which has been badly broken. It is not really strong enough to use on a stem, but the bowl of a glass can be successfully bonded, particularly where there are many pieces and to use Araldite would be difficult. Polyvinyl acetate emulsion is well suited for an object that is small and where the glass is thin. One can reconstruct the object in a continual process, for with this adhesive the pieces can be held in place and no great pressure is needed to achieve a good joint. Obviously this adhesive can only be used where strength is not the main objective and where the object itself will not be subjected to continual handling.

Filling in missing areas on glass is another problem, for as yet there is no successful method and no guaranteed non-discolouring resin that is both easy to use and practical. Polyester resins could be a possibility as they are clear, but they are not easy to use. A mould must be made of the missing area and the resin cast and then fitted, which is rather complicated. Where there is a chip missing or a hole right through the glass it is sometimes possible to fill this by stopping off one side with Sellotape and pouring the resin in to fill the aperture. One would have to carefully balance the glass so that the polyester resin is poured to the same level as the surface of the glass. Once set, surplus resin can be trimmed off and if necessary filed down. Fine abrasive paper and polishing with Solvol Autosol would complete the surface finishing.

The only resin that appears to be non-discolouring is the American Maraset type A655, but its use is limited as it must be heat cured at 70° centigrade. This means that pieces would have to be cast and then fitted to the object which is often difficult and time consuming. One can cast thin sheets of the resin successfully which can then be cut and fitted. The sheet must be stoved at 70° centigrade for sixteen hours and allowed to cool in the oven and the approximate shape can then be cut out with a fine saw blade. At this stage the sheet of resin will be flat, but if re-subjected to heat in the oven it will become pliable and can be bent while still warm to the correct shape which it will retain on becoming cool again. It can then be trimmed and filed down until it fits perfectly into the aperture where it can be bonded into place with either Araldite or a polyvinyl acetate emulsion. As it has a very glass-like appearance, little surface finishing will be required except perhaps a final polish with Solvol Autosol. A very successful repair can be achieved by using the resin in this way, but as it is not easily available and is expensive it may not be practical for the individual to consider.

JADE AND CORAL
Both these materials can be bonded with Araldite; in the case of jade, with no pigment added; for coral a matching colour can be made up with the resin and dry pigment to disguise the joint. If thought necessary dowels can be incorporated made from either stainless steel or glass. A glass dowel will always be preferable for jade, for being quite a transparent material a metal dowel would be visible as a dark shadow. A diamond point will be needed to drill the holes as both materials are hard and this should be carried out under water in the same manner as for ceramics or glass.

On jade, any small missing areas such as chips can be filled with Araldite without any pigment added as its slight yellow tint will take on the tone of the jade. One should use the grade AY103/HY951 or 956 of Araldite and not the two-tube variety. Missing chips on coral can be filled with the same resin but coloured to a matching tone with pigment. The polyvinyl acetate solid could also be used if the materials and equipment are available or a Cosmolloid wax and Ketone 'N' resin mixture with pigment would enable one to achieve a good result. The latter is detailed under the heading for alabaster.

IVORY
This material should never be cleaned with water as it will cause the ivory to warp. White spirit applied with cotton wool swabs should be used instead and this will remove most dirt. A polyvinyl acetate emulsion adhesive will bond ivory very well where necessary and can

72

either be held whilst setting or, if the ivory is inlay, it can be clamped or placed under weights to keep it flat. Missing areas, pins and dowels should always be carved wherever possible out of ivory rather than using a synthetic resin. Being a natural oily material in its natural state, if an ivory object is rather dry it can be rubbed with oil of almond which will restore some of its former surface quality. Ivory should not be displayed in direct sunlight as this will bleach it and the extreme heat may cause it to warp and split.

Where an object has split and there is a gap, it would be unwise in most cases to try to pull the two sides together, particularly where a considerable amount of strain would be put on the object. A very tiny split can probably be pulled together using polyvinyl acetate emulsion to secure a bond, but a much wider gap should not be forced if it will not close easily. and to fill would be the wiser remedy. Once split in one place the ivory is not likely to split elsewhere and one could either insert a new piece of ivory or fill with lightly coloured Araldite putty or a wax resin mixture. The Araldite should be tinted to tone in with the surrounding ivory, but as this resin is a much harder material than the ivory one should use it with discretion. Missing fingers, hands and other items should always be carved in ivory and fitted on, staining them if necessary to tone in with the original.

TERRA COTTA
For cleaning, cotton wool lightly damped with water and applied on a stick will be effective for removing surface dirt. It is essential to have the cotton wool swab damp rather than wet as the terra cotta is absorbent and the dirt could get drawn in if one is not careful. For more stubborn dirt ammonium acetate applied in the same way or with a brush will work well. This can be made up from a solution of acetic acid and ammonia mixed together until a neutral pH reading is reached. It should be wiped off the object with acetone.

Smaller objects can be bonded with a polyvinyl acetate such as Evo-stik Resin 'W', and larger breaks with Sintolit. Both adhesives can be held whilst setting and can be used on the same object where there are both large and small breaks. Dowels should be bonded in with Sintolit which will give the stronger bond. Missing areas can be filled in with Polyfilla which has been matched to the colour of the object with dry pigment; the same can be used for modelling up fingers, hands or other areas and where necessary stainless steel dowels and supports can be used.

Rowney Cryla colours are excellent for retouching and will dry with a fairly dull finish suitable for terra cotta. Rowney also make a matt or gloss finish medium which can be added to the colours if a slightly different effect is required.

ALABASTER
As with ivory, alabaster should never be cleaned with water as this will destroy the surface. White spirit will remove surface dirt quite

adequately. Alabasters are frequently painted and although white spirit will in most cases be quite safe to use, a test patch should be cleaned first just to make sure that no damage can occur. Large breaks can be bonded with Sintolit, using dowels of stainless steel if necessary, and polyvinyl acetate emulsion will be suitable for small breaks and chips.

A very good filling for alabaster is a mixture of Cosmolloid 80H wax and Ketone 'N' resin. The proportions are one part of Cosmolloid wax to two parts of Ketone 'N'. The resin is melted slowly over heat and the wax is added and combined. If the wax is in lump form it can be grated to help it melt more quickly, but this wax is also available in bead form which is very convenient. One should be very careful when melting wax as it is highly inflammable and should never be left to melt by itself. It is a sensible precaution to melt the resin and wax in a tin inside another container such as a saucepan which is filled with water, and one should not mix up too large a quantity at a time. This may take a little longer but is considerably safer. When the two ingredients are melted they should be poured out of the tin to form a sheet which is a more manageable way in which to to use it. A tray or shallow container is lined with silicone paper and the wax resin is poured in carefully but quickly before it begins to solidify. When cold, small pieces can be broken off the slab as required. A heated spatula or a tool heated over a spirit burner is used to apply the resin into the area to be filled. It is easier to melt the resin into the area with the tip of a heated tool, or one can place a little in a teaspoon, hold it over the flame and when melted pour quickly into the cavity. The filling is thus built up to the correct level and a final surface can be achieved either by using a heated spatula with silicone paper between it and the wax resin or by smoothing it down with white spirit on a piece of rag.

Cryla colours can be used if any retouching should be necessary.

MARBLE

For a marble object that is covered with surface dust or dirt a simple cleaning with water will probably be sufficient. Damp cotton wool swabs should be used rather than a scrubbing brush. Where the dirt is more stubborn the object should first be degreased with Nitromors and acetone which at the same time will remove a certain amount of grime. The Sepiolite pack method as described in the section on cleaning agents can then be employed to draw out the remainder of the dirt. Many marble objects will also respond to cleaning with Solvol Autosol. Applied with a stencil brush in a circular motion this will remove most ingrained dirt. The residue paste should be swabbed off with white spirit.

A protective surface coating for marble can be made up with Cosmolloid 80H wax and Ketone 'N' resin, this time in the proportion of two parts Cosmolloid wax to one part resin, with white spirit or Shellsol A to dilute it to a creamy consistency. This is applied to the cleaned marble with a soft brush making sure of complete coverage of the surface. Any excess is wiped off with a clean cloth and the object is finally dusted over with French chalk.

The best adhesive to use for marble is Sintolit, making sure that it is kept well within the perimeter of the break edge because of its discolouration; also any dowels to be used should be of stainless steel as this will not corrode. Marble powder can be mixed with polyvinyl acetate emulsion for filling, but one should always use a stainless steel or palette knife as the polyvinyl acetate will corrode other metals and cause the filling to discolour.

CHAPTER THIRTEEN
Case Histories

CASTING A CUP HANDLE

An identical cup, undamaged, was available from which to take a mould thus making the restoration task more simple. It is much easier to make a cast of a handle with a two-piece mould, which means that although it may involve a more complicated process to make the mould, the cast itself will be near perfect and easy to extricate from the mould which parts in two halves.

The cup handle is divided into two equal halves, one of which is blocked off with Plasticine as shown in the first picture of the series. A lump of Plasticine is rolled out to not less than a quarter to an inch thickness and pressed on to the side of the handle, blocking the apertures and forming a wall along the entire length of the handle. There should be no gaps between the Plasticine and the ceramic for the moulding material, in this case latex, to creep down into. A metal spatula can be used to smooth the Plasticine ensuring that there is contact all the way round. Holes can be pressed into the Plasticine wall to form keys for the two halves of the mould. A coating of latex is painted over the whole area using cotton wool rolled round the end of a stick. Any air bubbles that appear should either be blown or pricked with a pin, for it they are allowed to remain they will spoil the mould and the cast will be blemished. A quantity of latex is then mixed with cotton flock to form a paste consistency and this is laid over the whole pre-coated area to a depth of approximately a quarter of an inch, keeping the thickness as uniform as possible. The cup can be turned on its side for this operation so that the paste is applied to a horizontal surface and any tendency for it to slide is avoided. This layer of latex and flock is left to set for around twenty-four hours or less if the room is warm, and as it sets it will turn a brown colour.

76

 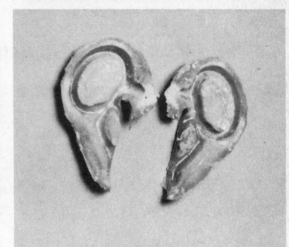

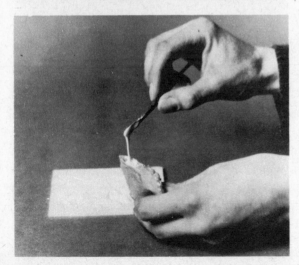 

77

When fully set, the Plasticine is removed from the other side making sure that no traces are left on the handle that could spoil the mould. If the latex exposed by the Plasticine still has a milky appearance it should be left for a few hours to complete curing. The outer edge of the half mould can be trimmed with scissors if it is at all ragged with thin strands of latex. Before the second half is applied a separating agent will be required to prevent the new half from sticking to the already cured latex. For this, Vaseline can be used applying it with a cotton wool-tipped stick and smearing it over the surface of the cured latex. One must be sure that the Vaseline covers every point where the two mould halves will be in contact or they will not part cleanly. Care must be taken not to smear the exposed half of the cup handle with Vaseline, and if this does happen it must be wiped off or it will spoil the surface of the cast. When the separator has been applied, the second half of the mould is made following exactly the same procedure as before. One coat of latex is painted on to cover the entire surface and then the latex and flock paste is laid on evenly and left to cure thoroughly. An outer casing of plaster of Paris can be made at this stage if it is thought necessary, but this would generally only apply where the mould was of a much larger handle and there was a possibility of distortion.

In this instance, being a small handle, the mould was considered to be quite rigid enough. The two mould halves were removed from the handle and dusted with French chalk. These two pieces must be joined together and sealed for the cast to be poured, and this was done with the aid of a rubber band and more latex. The two halves were linked together using a rubber band to hold them in position and the joint painted over with latex to form a seal, then left for an hour or so for this thin coating to set. A quantity of Araldite AY103/HY951 was made up and white pigment ground in to make a smooth consistency. The mould was then filled using a spatula to introduce the Araldite in a thin stream into one of the open ends. By filling slowly, any air that may be present inside the mould is expelled easily.

When the mould is filled it is supported in a sandbox until the Araldite has set hard. Using a sharp scalpel blade, the sealing skin of latex is slit and the two halves of the mould are parted. The Araldite cast is eased out and inspected for any blemishes. There may be a slight cast line down to the centre which will need rubbing down. The cast is then trimmed to fit the remainder of the handle on the cup and for this a hacksaw blade is used to cut the cast to the approximate size, and the ends are filed down until they correspond perfectly with the break edges on the cup.

To ensure a good strong bond, it was decided to dowel the cast to the cup. Holes were drilled into the handle remaining on the cup with a diamond point and in corresponding positions on the cast. Stainless steel rod was cut to size for the two dowels and the cup was supported in a sandbox in preparation for the cast to be bonded on.

78

Araldite with titanium dioxide was mixed up and introduced into the dowel holes and on to the break surfaces. The cast was fitted and the joints were tightly aligned using a strip of Sellotape stretched across the handle to either side of the cup to prevent any further movement. When the adhesive has set any excess Araldite is removed from the joints and the surfaces are adjusted until there is complete uniformity between the original ceramic and the cast.

Polyurethane PU 11 was used for retouching using a spray gun. The gold line down the centre of the handle was applied with gold leaf.

CHINESE PLATE

This plate had been repaired some years ago with rather unsightly-looking rivets. The face of the plate was very dirty along all the break edges and the old retouch had discoloured. The first job was to remove all the rivets and this was done with a hacksaw blade and a small pair of pliers. Very few rivets can be pulled straight out with pliers alone unless they have worked loose, which does not happen very often. The rivets are often bedded into the ceramic with a plaster composition and a swab of damp cotton wool placed over the area for a few minutes will soften this and help with extraction. Each rivet is sawn in half, keeping the blade in a horizontal position and taking great care not to make contact with the ceramic. Great patience has to be observed for this operation as if rushed, the glaze will get damaged by the saw blade and this would not be possible to rectify. When the rivet has been sawn through, a pair of pliers is used to twist round each half and gently pull them out of the ceramic. If the area has been damaged it should be easy to extract the rivet which must be pulled out vertically. If forced out at an angle the surrounding glaze could get chipped.

When all the rivets have been taken out, the rivet holes have to be cleaned and this is done with the aid of a diamond point under water until all the old composition has been removed, and on this particular plate some of these holes went right through to the other side. It is important for the edges of the rivet holes to be absolutely clean, for if not a shadow will be visible when they are filled in.

All the pieces of the plate were washed to remove surplus dirt from the surfaces and break edges and were then laid out on a sheet of polythene. In order to ensure perfectly clean joints, hydrogen peroxide on cotton wool swabs was applied to all the break edges and rivet holes to bleach out any remaining dirt. The swabs were left on for two hours and the process repeated until when placed together the break edges were virtually invisible. The pieces were thoroughly washed with water and left to dry; then the edges were wiped over with acetone in preparation for bonding.

Araldite AY103/HY951 was mixed with white pigment and a little colour to tone in with the blue grey of the plate which was then reassembled using Sellotape to pull the joints tightly together,

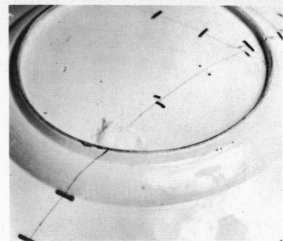

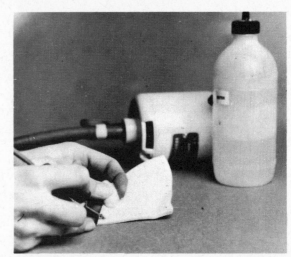

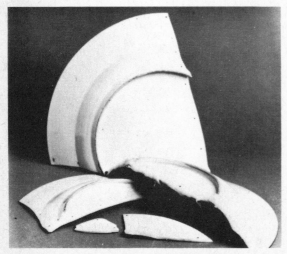

checking that all the break edges were perfectly aligned. The Sellotape was applied systematically front and back keeping the tensioning even so as not to pull any joints out of line. The plate was then left for twenty-four hours and when the adhesive had set the tape was stripped off the back. It was discovered that the enamel in some places on the front of the plate was being lifted by the tape, so instead of stripping off, the tape was soaked with white spirit and swabbed off thus avoiding unnecessary damage.

A lightly coloured filling was mixed up using Araldite AY103/HY951, pigment and kaolin and this was pressed into all the cavities and rivet holes. The filling was pressed little by little into the rivet holes, as air tends to get trapped if no escape is allowed for it and causes the filling to rise. When set hard, the fillings were rubbed down with abrasive paper and a second application of Araldite putty was required to make good the discrepancies. These fillings were in turn rubbed down and the surfaces worked until there was perfect uniformity with the surrounding ceramic. Both surfaces of the plate were given a final clean over with acetone to remove any traces of grease or dirt.

Polyurethane PU 11 mixed with dry pigment was used for retouching which was applied by brush, the background glaze being matched first and the coloured decoration added afterwards. The final surface to the retouch was achieved by polishing with Solvol Autosol.

PERSIAN PLATE

This large earthenware plate arrived in a badly broken state with most of the break edges in a very chipped condition. It had been repaired before more than once as there were rivet holes in most of the pieces and a great deal of adhesive was remaining on the break edges. There was also quite a lot of discoloured overpainting on the surface. All of this had

to be removed before the plate could be reconstructed and Nitromors was used to strip the old paint and remove the old adhesive. A sharp blade was needed to pick out some of the adhesive which was trapped in cavities and cracks.

When all the break surfaces were pefectly clean, a trial run had to be made to work out the procedure for bonding all the pieces together. It was discovered that the plate could be reconstructed in such a manner that one had two complete halves which could then be fitted together perfectly. It was therefore decided to bond the pieces of each half and then join the two together.

As there were so many pieces, Sintolit was used as the adhesive to enable each one to be held in place whilst setting, and Sellotape was also used where possible to assist in making sure each joint was tight and accurate. This plate was quite heavy and as the main centre break would possibly be subjected to a certain amount of strain, it was thought that if dowels were used between the two halves, this would ensure a really good bond. The points where the dowels were to be positioned were marked on one side with a blob of paint and the two halves brought together, thus indicating the exact spot on the opposite half, ensuring that the drilled holes would correspond. Three dowel holes were drilled into each half to a depth of about $\frac{3}{16}$ in. and with a diameter of just over $\frac{1}{8}$ in. The holes were drilled with a diamond point and the dowelling cut to size.

Araldite was used as the adhesive for this joint as the Sintolit would not allow time for adjustments. The adhesive was mixed up with a little pigment to tone with the body of the ceramic, and this was left on one side for a while until it became fairly tacky. A sandbox was prepared in which to balance the plate, and for this object a washing-up bowl was found to be just big enough. The adhesive was applied to the break edges and into the dowel holes, and the lower half of the plate was supported in the sand. The stainless steel rods were positioned and strips of wide Sellotape were stuck to the plate in advance. The two break edges were brought together into correct position and the tape drawn up and stretched over the break until the two halves were securely held together. The plate was then taken out of the sandbox and placed on the table and more strips of tape were applied, pulling very tightly across the joint on both the back and front of the plate. When the joint was judged to be perfectly aligned the plate was balanced back in the sandbox and left until the adhesive had set.

There were large areas that needed filling, particularly on the back including one piece of the rim which was missing. Polyfilla with pigment added was used for this job, and the fillings were applied as accurately as possible in the first instance in an attempt to reduce the amount of work that would be required in rubbing down. It was in fact only necessary to rub the fillings down once, and Fine Surface Polyfilla was used for the final layer with which a perfect surface was achieved for the retouch.

Polyurethane PU 11 was used for the retouching which was applied

by brush. An approximate colour was painted on first of all, with subsequent layers building up to a perfect match with the original glaze. For the back of the plate which was covered with fillings, it was decided to retouch with a colour that would blend in with the glaze but not be invisible. To achieve the latter would have meant spraying and as the fillings on one half of the plate were very close together, the retouched areas would probably have overlapped and too much of the glazed surface would have been covered. An approximate retouch, if very closely matched to the original can be very acceptable and in many cases preferable to an invisible retouch where the paint may be covering most of the surface.

CHINESE BOWL

This porcelain bowl had been badly bonded together and all the joints would have to be parted. The old adhesive was luckily water

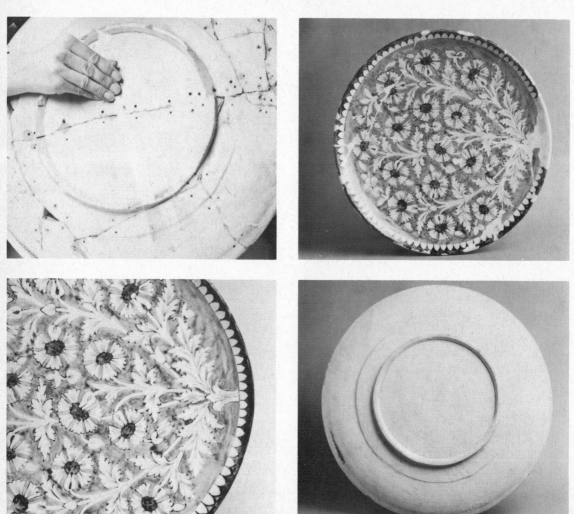

soluble, so that when the bowl was soaked in hot water for about an hour the joints parted company quite easily. The adhesive was removed from the break edges with cotton wool swabs, using a scalpel blade for more stubborn areas. The edges were wiped over with acetone and looked clean, but when fitted together there was a distinct line visible so it was decided that hydrogen peroxide should be used to bleach out the remaining dirt. The pieces were put in a shallow polythene container and strips of cotton wool were soaked in the peroxide solution and placed along all the break edges. They were left for about two hours and then replaced with more swabs, and this process was repeated three times until the edges were perfectly clean. The pieces were thoroughly washed and then wiped over with acetone and left to dry.

Araldite AY103/HY951 was used as the adhesive. Titanium dioxide and a little colour was mixed to give a basic tone resembling

the colour of the ceramic. A test run of the bonding sequence was made just using Sellotape and the two large pieces were joined first. The adhesive was applied to one break edge and the joint secured using tape to strap the two halves tightly together. It was decided to allow the adhesive to set before bonding on the other pieces, so the joint had to be perfectly aligned. The reason for this was that the remaining pieces of the bowl would fit in with no problem except that they would have to be very tightly strapped and it was feared that the tensioning required would pull the main joint out of alignment.

When this first section had set hard, the remaining pieces were fitted into place, each one being taped very tightly. With small pieces to fit in, it is essential that each one, when perfectly aligned, is taped in such a manner that it cannot be pulled out of true when tensioning Sellotape over from the following piece. The Sellotape was applied evenly and systematically both on the inside and outside surfaces of the bowl. When the adhesive was fully cured, the tape was removed and the chips and missing areas filled with Araldite putty. The Araldite had a little pigment added to provide a filling that would be of the same tone as the ceramic and be of assistance to the retouching. (One must be careful when toning a filling as the colour will darken considerably when the kaolin is added; one should therefore work initially very much on the light side.)

The filling, mixed to a stiff putty, was applied with a spatula, pressing well into the cavities, and was allowed to set hard. Abrasive paper was used to take the fillings down and as some were very small, particularly along the breaks, a further application of Araldite putty was required to remedy the discrepancies. The fillings were then rubbed down until perfect surfaces were achieved.

Polyurethane PU 11 mixed with artists' dry pigments was used for retouching and applied by brush. Several coats were applied, each being allowed to harden and then rubbed down before the correct match was obtained. The flower decoration was then touched in as were the blue bands. The double blue bands on the inner surface had a suspicion of gold between them, and this was applied first, using tablet gold which was allowed to harden and was then burnished before the bands were painted in. The retouching was given a final surface polish with Solvol Autosol.

GERMAN FIGURINE
This figurine, standing just five inches high, was broken in several places and the fingers on the woman's right hand were missing. The leg and foot of the man were bonded on with Araldite AY103/HY951, using a dowel at the knee joint. The foot was bonded on to the lower leg first of all and, when the adhesive had set hard, the main figure was bedded into a sandbox at the correct angle so that the leg could be balanced in position. Dowel holes had been drilled into both break surfaces using a diamond point, and the

86

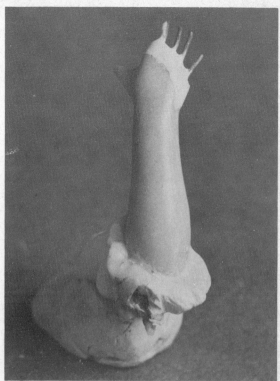

stainless steel rod cut to the correct length. A little Araldite with white pigment was placed into the very bottom of the holes, on the break surfaces and on both ends of the steel dowel. An Araldite putty was mixed up and packed into both dowel holes allowing room for the dowel itself, which was then placed into position in the bedded half of the figurine. The leg was then fitted and with a little pressure the two break edges were aligned. A strip of Sellotape and a wedge of Plasticine were employed to prevent the joint from moving out of true, and the object was left until the adhesive had set hard.

Meanwhile the broken arm was bonded together using a block of Plasticine in which to bed the upper arm while the forearm was balanced in position. As the hand was so small, about a quarter of an inch long, it was decided to model up the fingers before the arm was bonded on to the main figure as this model would allow considerably more freedom whilst working. Araldite, titanium dioxide and kaolin were mixed to a suitable consistency and the fillings required on the main figure were attended to first. It being such a small object, the fillings were applied as accurately as possible at the first attempt as it would be very trying to carry out a great deal of rubbing down on the areas that were extremely difficult to get at.

The hand was too small to allow for dowel holes and so the break was lightly scored with a diamond point to provide a key, and a block of Araldite putty was applied in the approximate shape of the knuckle area. This was allowed to reach a rubbery, semi-set state and then supporting wires for the fingers were inserted into position. Fuse wire was used, as the fingers were so minute and it would be much easier to build them up around a support rather than attempting to model them without. Before inserting, the end of each finger wire was dipped in Araldite, without kaolin, to ensure that they would bond into the putty accurately. When the wires were set hard in position the fingers were modelled up with Araldite putty which was applied layer by layer, gradually building up each finger accurately so as to avoid too much rubbing or carving down. When set hard, the hand was rubbed down with abrasive paper, narrow strips of which were drawn up and down between the fingers to surface the areas. Other fillings on the rest of the figure were also surfaced ready for retouching.

In view of the position that the hand would be in when attached to the figurine, it was decided that for convenience it should be retouched before it was bonded on. Polyurethane PU 11 with dry pigment was used and this was applied with a spray gun. A light base colour was mixed up first, thinned to the correct consistency and applied in an even layer being careful not to extend the retouch too far over the edge of the filling. When hardened, this was gently rubbed down and the next layer which matched the flesh tint was sprayed on. The final application was transparent with a slight tint which linked up with the tone on the rest of the forearm. After being

88

left for two days to allow the polyurethane to harden, the arm was then bonded on to the figure. Dowel holes had been drilled and exactly the same procedure as used for the leg was followed. One or two very small fillings were required around the joint and these were made good with Araldite putty. The figurine was then retouched where required using polyurethane and dry pigments applied with a brush.

GREEN GLAZED EARTHENWARE BOWL

This bowl was broken in twelve pieces with only one missing area on the rim. The break edges were in fairly good condition with only a few bad chips, but some of the glaze had sheered off leaving ragged edges to some of the pieces. The broken pieces were reconstructed using Sellotape as a support to work out the sequence in which it should be put together. It was noted that most of the break edges

located well together and did not need any adjusting to form tight joints, and for this reason it was decided to bond the bowl together with a polyvinyl acetate emulsion adhesive which would be quite strong enough. The bowl had been previously broken and bonded to gether with a water soluble adhesive, and to remove this, cotton wool swabs soaked in warm water were placed along the break edges to soften the glue sufficiently for it to be wiped off easily. When all the old adhesive had been removed the edges were given a final cleaning with acetone. Bonding was carried out in the sequence decided on at the trial run. The break edges were slightly damped before the adhesive was applied and the two pieces brought together and pressed tightly to secure a perfect close joint. Sellotape was used as an added support for the pieces, tensioning it where necessary. The bowl was gradually built up with the last two pieces being fitted together continually checking each joint for accuracy.

One should allow ten minutes or so between bonding on each piece for the adhesive to set sufficiently, and applying strips of tape across each joint will help to ensure that they do not part if pressure is needed to fit the following piece tightly. Once fully set, the tape is removed, and any adhesive that has been squeezed out on to the surface can be taken off with a sharp blade.

Polyfilla, with pigment added to match the body colour of the ceramic was used for filling in the chips around the breaks and the missing area on the rim. The base, which had quite a large area missing was made up with the same material, but care was taken not to alter the natural tilt of the bowl.

The fillings were carefully rubbed down and readjusted where necessary.

The blue-green glaze was fairly transparent and was matched up using thin layers of polyurethane PU 11 and dry pigments applied by brush. Transparent layers of paint were laid on top of each other allowing the polyurethane to harden and be rubbed down between each application. The glaze varied from a dense green to a pale turquoise colour and the retouching had to follow these alterations very accurately to blend in. The glaze also had a slightly crazed appearance and some of the lines were carried across the retouch to produce a uniformity. The retouched areas were polished with Solvol Autosol to achieve the final surface finish.

SOUTH AMERICAN POT

This painted earthenware pot had been broken in several pieces. The body of the ceramic was too porous to consider using Araldite even in a tacky state, so it was decided to use Sintolit and bond the object together at one session. Because of the painted surface it would not be possible to use Sellotape, so it was important to be able to hold the joints in place whilst the adhesive set. Tape could not be used either to assist in the trial run of reassembly so the pieces had to be carefully examined and a sequence worked our purely by eye to ensure that no pieces would be locked out. Having decided on the first piece to be bonded on, a small quantity of Sintolit was mixed and applied to one break edge with a spatula, keeping the bulk of the adhesive towards the inside edge so that it would be unlikely to be squeezed out on to the painted surface. With the main part of the object held in the left hand which was resting on the table, and the broken piece held firmly in the right hand, the two break edges were brought together, pressing tightly.

The two halves were wriggled very slightly so that they locked together, perfectly positioned so that there would be no further movement. They are then held under slight pressure until the adhesive has set which will take about ten minutes.

The object was thus pieced together, making sure each joint was as perfect as possible before the next was added. A careful check must be made as each piece has to be bonded on making sure that the following piece will not be locked out by the acute angle into which it cannot be fitted. In fact, one must be working and thinking at least a step ahead all the time, and on an object like this one, which was virtually formed in two units, one had to make sure that the two halves would link up perfectly when the final piece was bonded on.

One should also be careful when working on an object where the body tends to be crumbly, as in this case. Each break edge should be closely examined, brushing out any loose particles which could prevent a tight joint, before every bonding operation. Due care must also be observed when fitting the break edges together, for if they are grated rather than gently eased into position, flakes may break off and apart from the fact that this should not be allowed to happen, one will be involved in more work to repair the damage.

Having reconstructed the object, the next process was to fill the

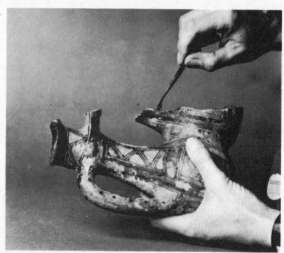
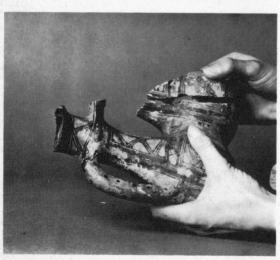

missing areas around the joints. This pot suffered considerably, since being a relatively low-fired earthenware, on the impact of dropping most of the break edges were badly chipped and crumbled off taking some of the paint at the same time. Polyfilla with a little pigment added to give an approximate tone, and mixed to a fairly stiff consistency, was used for the fillings. These were applied as accurately as possible at the first attempt as one would have to be extremely careful when rubbing down to avoid damage to the painted surface. One can achieve more accuracy if the Polyfilla is stiff rather than too wet. The abrasive paper was folded into small squares to provide more control over the rubbing down. Any areas that required it were refilled and a fine paper was used for the final surface finish. Cryla colours were used for the retouching as they gave the same surface appearance as the original paint.

The first application will tend to sink into the Polyfilla and become much darker, so an approximate colour, mixed very much on the light side, is painted on first and allowed to dry thus forming a sealing coat. The second layer is mixed to a perfect match, again allowing for fractional darkening as the paint dries; the main blocks of colour are then retouched in. The design, which in this case consisted simply of straight, chalky black lines, is painted on last of all. The Cryla colours will paint on in smooth even layers and there should be no need to rub down at all between applications. These colours are very stable, there being no need for a protective coating.

BLUE AND WHITE CHINESE VASE

This porcelain vase had been previously bonded together with an adhesive soluble in acetone, so it was a comparatively easy job to get the joints apart. Cotton wool swabs soaked in acetone and placed on the breaks were sufficient to soften the adhesive enough to allow the pieces to be gently pulled apart. All remaining adhesive on the edges was swabbed off thoroughly. There was some make-up with plaster and this was removed manually after being softened with water. A considerable amount of old repainting was stripped off the surface with Nitromors. To ensure good clean joints, all the break edges were finally treated with hydrogen peroxide applied on cotton wool swabs, and all the pieces were then thoroughly washed in water. Before bonding commenced, a trial run was made to work out the method of procedure to follow, using Sellotape to hold the pieces together. It was decided in this case that as one or two pieces had sprung, by bonding together in one attempt a more successful job would be achieved. Araldite AY103/HY951 mixed with titanium dioxide and a little colour to tone in with the blue-grey glaze was used for bonding.

Being a fairly large object of sixteen inches in height the wider Sellotape was selected for strapping as considerable tensioning would be required to pull the sprung pieces into line. In one way, a large object like this is easier to deal with as when standing up one can

apply more pressure while still keeping a good grip on the object. Applying pressure with one hand requires a lot of strength, and one needs to be well balanced enough not to allow the object to slip. When strapping up an object of this size it would be very wise to make sure one is aware of the breaking point of the Sellotape or a disaster could occur.

The areas that needed making up were mostly on the perimeter of the rim of the neck, and as there would be no adverse effect on the rest of the tightly strapped vase, it was decided to put the basic fillings into these areas at this stage. The remaining adhesive was mixed to a stiff putty consistency with kaolin powder, keeping a little Araldite without the filling on one side to paint on the break edges in order to provide a good bond between the ceramic and the putty. A double layer of Sellotape was positioned on the inside of the neck to form a support for the filling, and the putty was applied with a spatula, as neatly as possible. Further strips of tape were laid across the front of the filling to prevent sagging. The object was then left for two days to allow the Araldite to cure fully.

The Sellotape was then peeled off and excess adhesive along the break edges was removed with a scalpel blade. An Araldite putty was mixed up and further chips and larger areas were filled as accurately as possible; at the same time the made-up areas on the neck were inspected and any discrepancies were adjusted. When fully set, a file was used to get the overfilled areas down to a reasonable level and then abrasive paper to smooth down the grooves left by the file. More discrepancies found on the fillings at this stage were made good with Araldite putty. The rubbing down process continued until the finger tip, when run across, could determine no difference between the made up areas and the surrounding ceramic. To ensure that the fillings were up to standard a thin coat of white pigment and polyurethane was sprayed on to them. (By doing this the slightest blemishes will show up and these can then be remedied before final retouching.) The fillings on the rim of the vase covered quite a large area so it was decided to spray these both on the inside and outside surfaces, using polyurethane PU 11 as the retouching medium. Over large areas like these, it is preferable to spray as one can get a much more even layer of paint immediately and the amount of overspray on to the surrounding glaze can be kept to an absolute minimum. An approximate colour, slightly lighter than would be required finally, was sprayed on to provide a base, and smaller areas of background colour were retouched with a brush. This was given two days to harden enough to be lightly rubbed down before the next layer was applied; and the process was repeated until a final matching colour was achieved. Small areas along the break edges were all retouched in with a brush, again rubbing down between each application until the final surface was reached. Solvol Autosol provided the final polish to the retouching.

LID OF A DERBY POT-POURRI

Areas of the open-worked rim around the lid of this pot-pourri were missing in three places. Rather than model up free hand, which would take far too long, it was decided to make moulds on areas of the rim that were complete. Rubber-latex emulsion was chosen as the material from which to make the moulds, and in order to prevent the latex from travelling too far through the holes, a block of Plasticine was placed across the underside of the lid. One should allow a margin of Plasiticine round the perimeter of the area being moulded as this will provide a support for the latex.

Having cleaned the area thoroughly with acetone, a pre-coat of latex was applied to the surface of the ceramic using cotton wool on a stick and making sure that no air bubbles were trapped in the holes. The latex was carried on to the ridge of the lid in order to make the fitting of the mould over the missing area more secure. Latex emulsion was then mixed with cotton flock to form a paste consistency which was applied on top of the pre-coated area with a spatula, pressing down well into the holes and keeping the overall thickness even. The lid was then left for twenty-four hours to ensure the latex had cured.

It was decided to make a plaster of Paris support on the mould to provide extra rigidity and to prevent any chance of distortion. The plaster support must always be made before the mould is removed from the object. On a small area such as this, the plaster can be applied straight on to the latex, but on a casing that may be made of more than one section that may have more complicated contours, it would be wise to use a wet clay as a separator between the two materials. When the plaster support had set, it was levered off and the rubber mould eased off and checked for any blemishes and dusted with French chalk.

The mould, placed in its support, is then positioned on to the lid making sure that the pattern of the holes links up with the negatives on the mould. Sellotape will hold the mould in place and to make absolutely sure that the surfaces are making contact, it can be wedged from underneath with a block of Plasticine which will also hold the object in a horizontal position for filling. (The lid in the illustrations is at an angle purely for photographic purposes.)

Araldite AY103/HY951 was mixed with titanium dioxide to provide a white colour and a small amount was applied to the break edges of the ceramic and once coated was painted on to the surface of the mould. The remainder of the Araldite was mixed up to a putty consistency with kaolin and was pressed into the mould, little by little, taking care not to cover completely the top of what would be the holes, and this was then left to set hard. The plaster was removed and the rubber carefully eased off the cast which was then prepared for retouching. A round needle file was useful to grind out the holes so that they were all uniform; to smooth the inside surfaces, abrasive paper rolled up tightly was drawn back and forth through

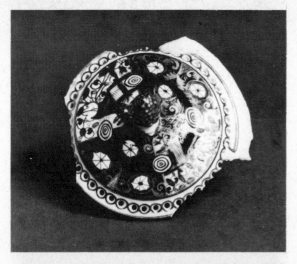

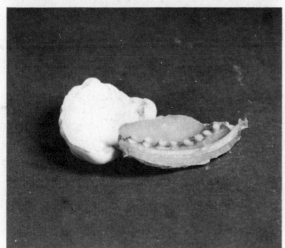

each hole until there were no remaining blemishes. The overall surface was rubbed down with a medium abrasive paper and finished with a much finer grade. Most of the rubbing down was required on the underside of the lid, and apart from some refilling required at the joints between the cast and the ceramic very little surfacing was needed on the face of the lid.

To check that the filling surfaces were perfect, the area was sprayed with polyurethane and white pigment and any further blemishes were adjusted. For retouching polyurethane PU 11 with dry pigments was used, and an initial white base was sprayed on and then further coats with a warm tone were applied to match the glaze of the ceramic. Each coating was allowed to dry hard and was rubbed down before the next was applied; the final surface was left for two days before the gold was applied. The pattern of the gold was very simple and it was decided to use gold tablet which could be painted on with a brush. After the gold was applied, it was left to set hard and was then burnished with an agate burnisher. On one or two places where the gold had missed, more was added and burnished down as before.

WEDGWOOD TEAPOT

Apart from new breaks on this object, there were also old ones where a cellulose adhesive had been used. This was either Durofix or something similar which was readily soluble in acetone. Cotton wool swabs soaked in this solvent were placed over the break edges to soften the adhesive; this was then removed with more cotton wool swabs and a blade for the more stubborn spots in the deeper cavities.

A test run was made of the sequence of reconstruction and it was decided to bond the main body of the teapot together first, adding the spout and handle after this had set. The spout which fitted very loosely into the aperture would need some fillings around the break edges on both itself and the main area on the teapot and would need to be supported whilst setting.

Araldite AY103/HY951 with titanium dioxide was used as the adhesive. The main pieces were fitted together, strapping each joint tightly as some pieces had sprung slightly out of true. As the ceramic was quite thin it was possible to pull these joints together without too much difficulty with the aid of Sellotape. The main body was then left for the adhesive to set hard, when the bonding tape was stripped off and preparations were made for bonding on the spout. The teapot was supported in a sandbox at the correct angle for the spout to maintain its balance. Sellotape was placed across the aperture on the inside of the teapot, and Araldite mixed with titanium dioxide was smeared on to the break edges. The spout was placed in position and a wedge of Plasticine was used as an extra support. Araldite with pigment and kaolin added to a firm consistency was used to fill the gaps around the break edges, and this was left to set hard, checking that the object was safely balanced in the sand.

98

The handle which was in four parts was then bonded on. The two end pieces were attached first to the teapot, again bedded in the sandbox. They were balanced in position with strips of tape and Plasticine employed as extra supports to prevent the joints moving out of true. Any inaccuracy would mean difficulty in aligning the remaining pieces. When the adhesive had set, the two middle pieces were fitted in. Araldite was applied to the centre break edges and the two parts were taped together. More adhesive was put on the other break edges and the two taped pieces were fitted into position. Sellotape was stretched over the length of the handle to hold the pieces together making sure that the break edges were accurately aligned.

When the adhesive had set, Araldite, white pigment and kaolin were mixed to a stiff putty consistency for the fillings and modelling up the missing area at the base of the handle. The fillings were rubbed down with abrasive paper taking care not to scratch the glaze. The teapot was retouched by brush with polyurethane PU 11 mixed with dry pigments.

VENETIAN GLASS

The stem of this glass was broken in one place just above the base. The break itself although clean was at a steep angle and if simply bonded, it would have been extremely difficult to prevent either half from slipping whilst the adhesive was setting. The stem was of a large enough diameter to allow for a dowel which would hold both the two halves in position whilst bonding and provide extra strength to the joint.

A diamond point was employed for drilling the dowel holes, with water constantly dripping on to the glass and the drill point. The holes could, of course, have been drilled with the glass entirely under water. (The depth and diameter of the dowel hole will depend on the dimensions of the object, but sufficient margin must be left round the hole so that the stem is not weakened.)

100

Glass rod was used for the dowel itself and in this case had to be ground down a little in order for it to fit comfortably. A diamond point was used for the grinding down and the rod was cut to the correct length with a diamond disc. The two break edges were cleaned with acetone to remove any grease that may have got on to the surface due to handling. Araldite AY103/HY951 was used as the adhesive and a small amount was introduced into both holes making sure that it covered the entire surface. A little adhesive was also smeared on to the break edges and to the glass rod which gave it back its clear appearance. It was then decided to stand the glass on its rim for bonding the two halves together as it was easier to judge the accuracy of the vertical position of the base when the glass was this way up. The dowel was placed in position and the two halves of the glass were then fitted together, twisting round a little to squeeze the adhesive out to a thin layer and to locate the correct

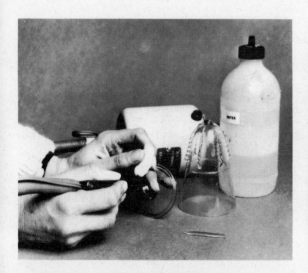

position of both halves, which when found locked together.

With a well-fitting internal dowel, the two halves are not likely to move out of line, but a strip of Sellotape taken from one side of the glass up over the base and down the opposite side will ensure that no movement can take place. The object was then left for the adhesive to set hard, the tape taken off and excess Araldite removed with a sharp blade.

BACKING A PANEL OF TILES

The problem may arise where it is necessary to back a set of tiles for display as a panel. In the past, panels of tiles have been attached to wooden backings with copper wires or simply plastered down on to wood, and they eventually either work loose and become unsafe or the old repairs begin to disintegrate or badly discolour. When they reach this state it is usually necessary to carry out a full restoration and also re-backing. The panel of tiles were in this condition, and these had been attached to their wooden backing with copper wires that were stapled to the back of each tile and threaded through and tied behind the wood.

Before work was begun each tile was numbered with a sticky label to help with reassembly (such numbering is best done in sequence from left to right starting with the top row). To release the tiles, the panel was laid face down on several layers of foam rubber to protect the front, and each wire was cut with tin snips and drawn out, thus releasing each tile. The backboard was lifted off and the tiles turned face upwards. The border round this particular panel had been made up from tiles of three different designs and the centre five main tiles on the top row below this border had been at some time cut in half. As the photograph shows, in order to incorporate these half tiles the border followed round the shape made by these and a wooden board was inserted in order to straighten the top for framing the whole panel. It was decided that as the border possibly did not originally belong and that as the design was not consistent they should be rearranged to form a straight line and the five half tiles would be built up to their original size. This rearrangement can be seen in the photograph at the end of the series.

Each tile was thoroughly cleaned, stripping off old retouch with Nitromors and removing poor fillings. Any broken tiles that had been badly stuck together were taken apart, the joints cleaned and were rebonded with Sintolit. As the backing is done with the tiles face down on the table, each one should have its number written on the back with a chinagraph pencil. This will help to ensure that the tiles are in the correct order when turned over on to their faces. If the number is placed in the top left hand corner of each tile one will also be sure of their being the right was up. Taking one row of tiles face up, they would be numbered from, for example, one to nine from left to right. When turned over for backing, they will read, from left to right, nine to one, and so on, being the complete reverse

of when they were face up. Numbering the back of the tiles may sound logical, but simple precautions are not always apparent at the time and mistakes have been made with tiles mysteriously turning upside down before this procedure became the rule. This method of displaying panels, using a polyurethane expanding foam as the backing, was devised after a great deal of trial and error and since this particular panel was done some slight adjustments have been brought in to overcome some of the problems that occur, and these are mentioned throughout the chapter.

Having decided how this particular panel was to be finally arranged, a large sheet of polythene was laid down over the table and the tiles in correct order placed face down. A wooden frame was made to enclose the tiles and hold them in position and, as this was too large for a cramp to be used, the corners had to be screwed together. The polythene was drawn up between the frame and the tiles to prevent the foam backing from sticking to the wood. The frame should allow for the depth of the tiles plus a half to one inch for the backing. These measurements will depend on the size of the whole panel and the strength and rigidity of the backing required. The polyurethane foam, made by Strand Glass, when expanded forms a rigid strong backing, light in weight and not liable to be affected by changes in humidity, and for these reasons it is ideal for panels of tiles.

The panel in question measured approximately 7ft × 4ft and each tile was much larger than the average size for tiles. It was decided to back the panel in one unit, as it would be difficult to divide it evenly into sections with the border tiles being so irregular in size. The space between each tile was filled in with Polyfilla to prevent the foam from creeping down and displacing the tiles. Polyfilla was also used to make up the missing tiles, and the panel was then left for two days to allow the filling to dry out. Sheets of expanded aluminium mesh were cut to cover the whole surface leaving a half inch margin all round the edge. This mesh is incorporated with the foam for additional reinforcement. Wooden blocks are cut and placed one in each corner and at regular intervals round the border with two or three down the centre of the panel. These are to keep the mesh from rising with the foam to the surface and to provide keys into which the frame can be secured with screws. If the panel is being made up in more than one unit these blocks of wood are essential for linking the sections together. In this case, their positioning must be the same on each panel, and in order to prevent them being moved by the foam they can be stapled to the aluminium mesh. Before the foam is poured, two or three large sheets of heavy glass should be covered in polythene in preparation for laying across the frame and keeping the surface of the foam level. The Strand Glass foam expands to approximately twenty times its original volume and is mixed in a fifty-fifty ratio of resin to catalyst. Disposable paper cups specially made for measuring out resins are available from Strand Glass and these, being marked in units by volume are ideal to use for mixing the foam in. The two components of the foam are measured out in separate cups and then poured together into another container, stirred vigorously with a palette knife for fifteen seconds and immediately poured on to the tiles at one end of the panel. The foam will start to rise within a further twenty seconds and the sheet must be placed across the frame to keep the surface level and to force the foam to travel along the tiles and through the mesh. A weight placed on top of the sheet of glass will ensure that it is not pushed out of position by the force of the foam. Even when the expansion has finished, the glass should be left in place for at least an hour.

Meanwhile, one can pour another section of foam at the opposite end of the panel using exactly the same procedure as before. When the sheet of glass is removed, the polythene coating should be examined in case it has been torn and if so it should be recovered or the foam will stick to the glass. More sections of foam can then be poured until the whole panel is backed. When all the foam has fully set, the panel can be turned over so that it is face up, using a thick sheet of blockboard as a support whilst moving it to prevent any danger of bending. The panel can be left on the table or leaned up against a solid support as a precaution against warping. If the panel is of medium size it can be screwed straight back into its frame which will keep it rigid.

This particular panel which was made up from larger than average tiles did not show any tendency towards warping at all, but another panel of the same overall size, but made up with smaller tiles of the normal five inches square, did in fact warp showing that one would have to be careful when deciding on the size of each section.

Having checked to make sure that all the tiles were in their correct position, the panel was leaned against a solid support to make access easier for filling and retouching. Polyfilla was used for grouting between all the tiles and for all the necessary fillings. Surface finish to the Polyfilla was achieved with abrasive papers of a fairly fine grade. Polyurethane PU 11 mixed with artist's pigment was used for retouching and was applied with a brush. The grouting between the tiles was retouched in a neutral colour using a matting agent to dull the polyurethane and to prevent it catching the light.

As stated previously, warping can occur on a large oblong panel either due to the fact that it has been moved before the foam has had sufficient time to cure thoroughly, or because it has been leaned against an inadequate support and its own weight has caused it to bend. Large panels do present problems, and in general it is far better to divide them up into smaller units of no more than four by three feet, and to link them together. Any panels or sections larger than this should have wooden battens incorporated into the foam backing to ensure rigidity is maintained. There should be no difficulty in linking up smaller panels so long as the wooden blocks are placed in identical positions on each section thus enabling metal plates to be screwed across from one block to the other. Wooden blocks placed down the sides of the sections will also provide a solid area into which the frame can be screwed, and if triangular pieces are fitted into the corners, metal corner plates can be screwed on.

The polyurethane foam can be bought in quite small quantities and if one decides to use this backing method for the first time, it would be wise to do a test run through of the procedure using ordinary domestic tiles just to make sure that one is aware of all the problems that are likely to occur. The point where difficulties may arise is in the mixing and pouring of the foam which must be achieved in thirty to forty seconds, so one must make sure that all equipment required is well to hand. Should a mistake be made and the foam overflows it can easily be cut back with a saw blade or taken down with a coarse file or Surform. As with most restoration processes experience and practice will overcome most of the problems and make the task easier.

U.S. Suppliers' List

ABRASIVES
Norton Company, Coater Abrasive Division,
Troy, New York 12181

CASTING AND MOULDING
Maraset:
The American Marblette Corp.,
37-31 30th Street,
Long Island City, New York 11101

CHEMICALS
City Chemical Corporation, 132 West 22nd Street,
New York, N.Y. 10011

DE-IONISED WATER UNITS
From water-softener unit suppliers
also:
Continental De-ionised Water Service,
490 Hendricks Causeway,
Ridgefield, New Jersey 07657

DENTAL DRILLS
Health Co., Inc., 331 West 44th Street,
New York, N.Y. 10036

DIAMOND DRILLS
Foredom Electric Company, Route 6, Stony Hill,
Bethel, Connecticut 06801

FILLINGS
Barytes: See pottery and ceramic suppliers
Vinyl Reinforced Cellulose:
The Dap Corporation makes this in both
putty and powder form. They can be
obtained at local hardware stores.
Cotton Flock:
Plymouth Fibres Co., Traffic and Palmetto Streets,
Brooklyn, N.Y. 11227

GLAZE MATERIALS AND EQUIPMENT
American Art Clay Company, 4717 West 16th
Street, Indianapolis, Indiana 46222
Brodhead-Garrett Company, 4560 East 17th Street,
Cleveland, Ohio 44105
Gare Ceramic Supply, 165 Rosemont Street,
Haverhill, Massachusetts 01830

LISSAPOL
This is a brand name for a wetting agent available in
England. Similar wetting agents can be obtained from
chemical manufacturers in the U.S.

PAINTS AND ENAMELS
Stoving enamels:
ICI-North America Ltd. 444 Madison Avenue,
New York, N.Y. 10021
Artists dry colors:
Fezzandie and Sperrle, Lafayette Street,
New York, N.Y. 10003
Lustre colors:
The Mearl Corporation,
41 East 42nd Street,
New York, N.Y. 10017

PLASTICS, EPOXIES, RESINS
Araldite
Ciba-Geigy, 18 East 72nd Street
New York, N.Y. 10014
Polyvinyl Acetate Emulsion (PVA):
Union Carbide Plastics Co., 270 Park Avenue,
New York, N.Y. 10017
Polyester Resin:
Shell Chemical Co., Plastics and Resins Division,
110 West 51st Street, New York, N.Y. 10020
Other General Suppliers:
Shell Chemicals, Plastics Division,
110 West 51st Street, New York, N.Y. 10020
Taylor and Art, Inc., 1710 East 12th Street,
Oakland, California 94606
Industrial Plastics, 324 Canal Street,
New York, N.Y. 10013

POTTERY AND CERAMIC SUPPLIERS WITH MAIL ORDER SERVICE

American Art Clay Company, 2717 West 16th Street, Indianapolis, Indiana 46222

Denver Fire Clay Company, 3033 Blake Street, Denver, Colorado 80205

Seeleys Ceramic Service, 9 River Street, Oneonta, New York 13820

TOOLS

Allcraft Tool & Supply Co., Inc., 215 Park Avenue, New York, N.Y. 10017

Brodhead-Garrett Co., 4560 East 17th Street, Cleveland, Ohio 44105

L. H. Butcher Company, 15th and Vermont Streets, San Francisco, California 94103

The Craftool Company, Inc., 1421 West 240th Street, Harbor City, California 90710

Sculpture House, 38 East 30th Street, New York, N.Y. 10016

WAX

Will and Baumer Candle Co., Inc., Liverpool Road, Syracuse, New York 13200

OTHER EQUIPMENT

Ohaus, 29 Hanover Road, Florham Park, N.J. 07932

Patterson-Ludlow Division, Banner Industries, Ltd, 1250 Saint George Street, East Liverpool, Ohio 43920

Simpson Mix-Muller Division, National Engineering Co, Suite 2060, 20 North Wacker Street, Chicago, Illinois 60606

J. C. Steele and Sons, Company, 710 South Mulberry Street, Drawer 951, Statesville, North Carolina 28677

James Walker Corporation, Inc., 365 South First Avenue, East Duluth, Minnesota 55802

The following are the American equivalents of certain English terms used in the text which may not be familiar to American readers.

blockboard: homosote
builders' merchants: hardware store or lumber yard, according to the item needed
chemist: drugstore
French chalk: powdered chalk
ironmonger: hardware store
kaolin powder: kaolin flour
orange stick: toothpick
spray gun and compressor: airbrush
cellotape: scotch tape
washing up bowl: enamel or plastic kitchen sink bowl
chinagraph pencil: china marking pencil
aluminium: aluminum

MATERIALS AND SUPPLIES

As indicated in the text, most of the equipment and materials described can be found, according to their character, in hardware stores; lumber yards; artists', jewellers' and sculpture suppliers; laboratory, medical and dentists' suppliers; drugstores; chemical and plastics manufacturers and auto body repair shops. A short list of manufacturers of some specialized equipment, however, is given here. Beginners may wish to order from the list of British suppliers given in the appendix, until they gain confidence with their materials.

Equipment and Materials List

EQUIPMENT

DE-IONISED WATER UNITS – B113 ELGASTAT. B114 ELGACAN
Elga Products, Lane End, Bucks or F. W. Joel, 9 Church Manor, Bishop's Stortford, Herts

DENTAL DRILLS: SECO UNIVERSAL MOTOR
Buck and Ryan, 101 Tottenham Court Road, London W1 and dental equipment suppliers

DIAMOND DRILLS, PAINTS AND DISCS
Diamond Enterprises, 263-269 City Road, London EC1 or Dental suppliers such as Claudius Ash, 26 Broadwick Street, London W1

FILES AND RIFFLERS (CURVED)
E. Gray and Sons Ltd, Grayson House, 12-16 Clerkenwell Road, London EC1

GENERAL TOOLS (Files, Clamps, etc.)
Buck and Ryan, 101 Tottenham Court Road, London W1 or any good ironmonger

HEATED SPATULA
Willard Electrical Services, Industrial Estate, Chichester, Sussex

JEWELLERS' FILES AND TOOLS
A. Shoot and Sons Ltd, 85 Whitechapel High Street, London E1

METAL SPATULAS AND SCULPTURE TOOLS
Alec Tiranti Ltd, Goodge Place, London W1

PLASTIC BOTTLES AND CONTAINERS
Transatlantic Plastics Ltd, Fulham Road, London SW6

SCALPELS AND BLADES
Most good art shops and ironmongers

SPRAY GUNS AND COMPRESSORS
Colour Sprays Ltd, 26 Southwark Bridge Road, London SE1, or Conopois Instruments, Shoreham-by-Sea, Sussex

MATERIALS

ABRASIVE PAPER TRIMITE WET OR DRY
Silicon carbide abrasive paper available in various grades from coarse to very fine. From most ironmongers and tool shops, also John Myland Ltd, 80 Norwood High Street, London SE27 9NW

ARALDITE. GRADES AV100/HV100. AY103/HY951 or 956
Epoxy resins for bonding, filling and casting. Ciba-Geigy Ltd, Duxford, Cambridge. Two-tube variety which is the same as AV100/HV100 is available from most ironmongers.

ALUMINIUM MESH SHEETS 6 ft × 3 ft
From Farmers Bros, Fulham Road, London SW6 or any builders merchants

ALUMINIUM TAPE
Auto Wrappers Ltd, 110 Hammersmith Road, London W6

BARYTES POWDER. BLEACHED WHITE GRADE 1
Barium Chemicals, Widnes, Lancashire

BOSTIK QUICK SET ADHESIVE
Epoxy resin mixed in equal proportions. Sets in approx. 5-10 min. From ironmongers and Do-It-Yourself shops.

CHINTEX CLEAR GLAZE
Synthetic glaze medium stoved at 220°F for about one hour. Chintex, Mackall, Bristol, B819 1JZ

COSMOLLOID WAX, 80H
Rowney Ltd, 12 Percy Street, London W1A 2BP

COTTON FLOCK, WHITE
Fibre Products, Stavely Mills, Denholme, Yorkshire

CYANOLIT
Instant setting cyanocrylate impact adhesive. Tiranti Ltd, Goodge Place, London W1, and other art shops

DUTCH METAL (Substitute for Gold Leaf)
Rowneys, 12 Percy Street, London W1A 2BP and George Whiley, South Ruislip, Middlesex

EASTMANS 910
Instant setting cyanocrylate impact adhesive. Armstrong Cork Co. Kingsbury, London NW9

EVO-STIK RESIN 'W'
Polyvinyl acetate emulsion adhesive. Evode Ltd, Stafford, ironmongers, Do-It-Yourself shops, etc.

FLEX-I-GRIT A400/10/02
Very fine plastic backed abrasive sheets. F. W. Joel, 9, Church Manor, Bishop's Stortford

FRENCH CHALK
John Myland Ltd, 80 Norwood High Street, London SE27 9NW or Boots the Chemists

GIPGLOSS CELLULOSE THINNERS
General Industrial Paints, Wadsworth Road, Perivale, Middlesex

GLASS FIBRES, TAPES AND GAUZES
Strand Glass, 79 High Street, Brentford, Middlesex and F. W. Joel, 9 Church Manor, Bishop's Stortford, Herts

GOLD LEAF (TRANSFER) TABLET GOLD
George Whiley Ltd, South Ruislip, Middlesex, and Rowney and Winsor and Newton art shops

JENOLITE
In liquid or paste form for removing rust stains. A. Duckham, Jenolite Works, Rusham Road, Egham, Surrey. In tube form from most hardware stores

KAOLIN POWDER
Hopkins and Williams, Freshwater Road, Chadwell Heath, Essex or Boots the Chemists

KETONE RESIN 'N'
Synthetic resin based on polycyclohexanome. Soluble in white spirit. F. W. Joel, 9 Church Manor, Bishop's Stortford, Herts. Rowney, 12 Percy Street, London W1A 2BP

LISSAPOL NDB
Non-ionic detergent manufactured by Imperial Chemical Industries Ltd, and available from F. W. Joel, 9 Church Manor, Bishop's Stortford, Herts

MARAGLAS MARASET TYPE A 655
Colourless epoxy resin for casting and impregnating. Must be heat cured for 16-24 hours at 71° centigrade. Marblette Corporation, 27-31 Thirtieth Street, Long Island, New York, U.S.A.

MATTING AGENTS TK 800, HK 125
Bush, Beach, Segner and Bayley, Marlow House, Lloyds Avenue, London EC3 or F. W. Joel, 9 Church Manor, Bishop's Stortford, Herts

MELINEX FILM
Polyethylene terepthalate film. Obtainable in various thicknesses and manufactured by Imperial Chemicals Ltd, Plastics Division, Welwyn Garden City, Herts. Available from Boyden Data Papers Ltd, Trade Services Division, Camberwell, London SE5

MELINEX METAL FOIL
George Whiley Ltd, Victoria Road, South Ruislip, Middlesex HA4 OLG

MURANO REFLECTIVE COLOURS
For mixing with a retouching medium to produce a lustre effect. Cornelius Chemicals Ltd, Ibex House, Minories, London EC3

NITROMORS WATER WASHABLE OR SPIRIT
Non-inflammable paint remover based on methylene chloride. John Myland Ltd, 80 Norwood High Street, London SE27 9NW or most hardware or paint shops

PIGMENTS. ARTIST QUALITY DRY
Winsor and Newton, Rathbone Place, London W1 or C. Roberson and Co. Ltd, Parkway, London NW1 7PP

PARALAC STOVING ENAMEL
ICI Chemicals Ltd, Templar House, 81 High Holborn, London WC1

POLYFILLA. INTERIOR AND FINE SURFACE
A vinyl reinforced cellulose filler. Most hardware stores and builders merchants

POLYESTER CASTING RESINS
Tiranti Ltd, Goodge Place, London W1

POLYURETHANE FOAM (2 PACK)
Two-pack resin and isocyanate which are mixed in equal proportions and react forming a rigid polyurethane foam. Strand Glass, 79 High Street, Brentford, Middlesex

POLYURETHANE PU 11
Furniglas Ltd, 136-138 Great North Road, Hatfield, Herts

POLYURETHANE RUSTINS CLEAR GLOSS
Rustins Ltd, Drayton Works, Waterloo Road, London, NW2 and from hardware or paint shops

POLYVINYL ACETATE EMULSION. MOWLITH DMC 2
Harlow Chemical Company Ltd, Temple Fields, Harlow, Essex or F. W. Joel, 9 Church Manor, Bishop's Stortford, Herts

POLYVINYL ALCOHOL RHODOVIOL HS 100
R. W. Greef and Co. Ltd, Gresham Street, London EC2 or Rowneys, 12 Percy Street, London W1A 2BP

RUBBER LATEX EMULSION
For making flexible moulds. Bellman Ivey and Carter, 358A Grand Drive, Wimbledon, SW 20

SEPIOLITE 100 MESH
Hydrated magnesium silicate for drawing out stains.
F. W. Joel, 9 Church Manor, Bishop's Stortford, Herts

SILICONE PAPER
Rowneys, 12 Percy Street, London W1A 2BP

SILICONE RUBBER. SILASTOMER 9161. Cat
N9162
Tiranti Ltd, Goodge Place, London W1

SINTOLIT. TRANSPARENT AND WHITE
Cold curing, quick setting polyester adhesive. C.
Pisani, Carrara Wharf, Ranelagh Gardens, London
SW6

SOLVENTS AND CHEMICALS
Hopkins and Williams, Freshwater Road, Chadwell
Heath, Essex, and John Myland, 80 Norwood High
Street, London SE27 2NW and chemists

SOLVOL AUTOSOL
Fine abrasive paste for polishing and cleaning without
scratching. Solvol Lubricants Ltd, Reginald Square,
London SE8

STAINLESS STEEL DOWELLING
Renown Stainless Steel, 273 Green Lane, Palmers
Green, London N13

SWAB STICKS
Bell and Croydon, 50 Wigmore Street, London W1

TITANIUM DIOXIDE
John Myland, 80 Norwood High Street, London SE27
2NW and Winsor and Newton, Rathbone Place,
London W1

Index